The Future of Fathers
By
Rick McPhearson

Find Yourself a Mirror...

Take a look in the mirror and tell me what you see...
Are you truly the man and father that you really wish to be?
Are you a Father? Or are you failing?

Contents

About the Author
Written by Madison McPhearson

Introduction

Chapter One
Getting/Being Prepared

Chapter Two
Working on you….
The Man in the Mirror

Chapter Three
The Common Sense Effect

Chapter Four
Can We Talk?

Chapter Five
They Need You There

Chapter Six
Have No Fear

Chapter Seven
Friend or Father

Chapter Eight
Consistency through Challenges

Chapter Nine
Identity Crisis

Chapter Ten
Spiritual Guidance
Yours and Theirs

About the Author

By

Madison McPhearson

At a young age, I always loved and looked up to my father. I was confident in the relationship we had built and I always looked at him as the best daddy in the world (feel free to check all my homemade Father's Day and birthday cards for proof). I would see my dad every other weekend and I always loved it. I could always count on getting Round Table pizza for dinner on Friday and for sure an Oreo banana milkshake every night if I sweet talked him enough. I could also count on him yelling louder than pretty much any parent ever on the sidelines of my soccer games, and telling me afterwards, "You could've done way better." His own version of tough love is how I look back on it now. He never blew smoke up my ass, which is for certain. Another guarantee when I was really little, and didn't yet have my own taste in music, was the full-volume car sing-a-longs to BeBe and CeCe Winans, Kirk Franklin, and Donnie McClurkin.

I learned every word of course, so that I could sing with and sometimes we really would "sing like our parents were from Jamaica, our parents' parents were from Jamaica" and it was always a full-on, live, Super Bowl halftime show performance from the McPhearsons. I also remember the family camping trips, the trip to LEGOLAND and SeaWorld (all pictures of which have been burned because I was too fat for words), and lots and lots of BBQ's. During the summers it was pretty much always bring your kid to work day. Whether it was the Boys & Girls Club, Basketball Town, or Salvation Army, I was my dad's right hand woman at every event, every time. I grew up with kids who had far less than me and I experienced a lifestyle that had my dad work a "normal" job, I would never have been able to see. I played a lot. I am a Millennial, but I was an outside kid, my dad made sure of it. We rode bikes, went to the park, and I was always outside playing basketball or something with the neighborhood kids. We moved quite a bit too, into a few different houses, separated by a few different apartments. But the memories I have as a child going to my dad's house are nothing but positive and fun-filled times.

I remember the joy of being a kid and it felt very palpable with my dad. He made everything fun; if we were ever struggling financially I didn't feel it. All I knew was fun and the childlike wonder you are supposed to enjoy as a babe.

Well, flash forward to middle school and high school years. I suppose you're naturally supposed to start hating your parents and be a dramatic brat, otherwise did you even do it right? I suppose I may have taken this to a theatrical new level, but hear me out. Sometime at the beginning of my high school career, I found out my dad had cheated on my mom and that played a very big part in their divorce. Now, I barely even remember a time when my parents were not divorced, so I never had a hard time dealing with the divorce like a lot of kids whose parents split when they're in their formative years or whatever. I had come to terms with their living situation when I was around four so in the grand scheme of things, the divorce was meaningless to me. But, as a 14-year-old, to find out that my father cheated on my mom was earth-shattering. Later on, I found out that the woman he had an affair with was the woman we moved in with (along with her husband and two sons) for a short time while my dad was in the process of finding a different apartment. So not only was I deceived by my dad, but I played house with this woman, the woman who knowingly slept with a married man while she herself was married. To be honest, this still irks me, better yet it horrifies me, haunts me, ruins my psyche when it comes to trusting in a relationship, and most importantly it angers me to a point deep in my soul where I would go to jail for trying to kill this woman were I to see her again in public. Since the whole affair, in fact, I've seen her twice; once as a young child still and once around age 19. The only thing that stopped me from jumping over the counter at work and tackling her like a 400-lb linebacker is that exact work counter, and my desire to keep my job (also the fact that she was the size of a 400-lb linebacker and could've very well injured me instead). Anyway, I didn't end up killing this woman and I'm sure she will get whatever bad karma is coming her way.

Another part of this story involves a period where my dad and I had absolutely zero communication. Sometime either late sophomore or early junior year in high school, I got sick of going back and forth between parents' houses, and I felt that my dad was not taking care of me in a fashion that was acceptable to me when I was at his house. In addition to that, I hated my stepmom and she made the energy in the house absolutely horrible. Long story short, I wrote him a letter saying I did not want to see him anymore, go to his house every other weekend, or speak to him. Dramatic?

Yes, of course. But was it necessary for me? I believe so. For a year or two, I had no contact with my dad. I didn't even invite him to my high school graduation; when he showed up anyway I didn't speak to him. I had a lot of pinned up anger towards my dad, some rightfully directed and some not. I was a child and I didn't know how to express myself other than throwing a fit and that's kind of what I refer to it as my two year tantrum. But, as I said earlier, at the time, which was exactly what I needed in order to make peace with myself, my dad, my family situation, and just too peacefully get through high school. I don't regret anything and I think that those two years apart from my dad actually grew my appreciation for him and for the relationship that we now have.

Fast forward again to our current relationship: My freshman year of college, we mended fences and were able to come to a comfortable place with each other. It has been hard and there have been plenty of disagreements since we started talking again. I am certainly my father's daughter in the sense that we don't take anyone's shit. We are both so hard-headed and opinionated that our ideas tend to clash and oftentimes you'll hear us fighting for who can be the louder voice in the room. But that is the relationship we have and we work with it. We are in no way perfect, but we are in every way working for it. We are finally working for our relationship, our friendship, our compassion towards each other's opinions, our respect for each other; and all of that stems from how much we love each other. No matter what situation we were in, my father and I have always loved each other as vastly as the ocean is deep. I may not have always liked him, but I have always and will always love him (he told me that my whole life by the way: "You won't always like me Madison, but you will love me"). Ironic, huh? Anyway, that love is what keeps us so close. I call my dad just to tell him about my day. I know I can rely on him if I need to vent or if I just need someone to dog-sit. Despite the many bumps in the road and the many bumps to come, I know that

I have been blessed with an imperfect father who has a perfect love for me. And there is nothing more than an imperfect daughter with a perfect love for her father could ask for.

"Love is patient, love is kind. It does not envy, it does not boast, it is not proud. It does not dishonor others, it is not self-seeking, it is not easily angered, and it keeps no record of wrongs. Love does not delight in evil but rejoices with the truth. It always protects, always trusts, always hopes, and always perseveres. Love never fails." 1 Corinthians 13:4-8 (NIV).

Introduction

In January of 1997, my life changed when my daughter Madison was born into this world, a beautiful 7lb., 4oz. baby girl. Little did I know how much my life would change, or how many trials and tribulations I would have to endure to become the best father I possibly could. Then I thought is there such a thing as a good father, as I had no idea, being that I was raised by a single mom and never once had a dad in the home. For most of my life, I looked up to my oldest brother as my father figure, and honestly, I couldn't have had a better role model than my big brother, he was a man of integrity, honesty, and a strong work ethic.

On many occasions I would have to answer to him when I misbehaved, as mom was out doing what she needed to do for us to make ends meet. My family was a father by committee type family, meaning whomever mom left in charge was dad for the evening and if needed, he would take to your butt like he truly owned it. So to say I didn't have a father in my life is a true statement, however at the same time, I had five fathers, as I was the youngest of the six. Although they always made me feel loved and well taken care of, there was still something missing, I just felt like everyone else around me had the completeness of a family, and us, all we had was mom and each other.

I can't tell you the many times I would lie and make up stories about my dad whenever the conversation turned in that direction. My uncle Ed became my fictitious father and the stories just kept getting bigger and bolder. I mean me and my fictitious father had gone on some of the best camping, fishing, and weekend excursions a child could ever dream up. Not until one of my teachers that knew better over heard me lying about my father and called my mom did I stop bending truths and making up great stories. It was embarrassing when she called me out on it in front of the other students and made me tell the truth, then when I got home I had to endure the wrath of an angry mom that had taught us to be proud of who we were and how we were raised.

That's when it hit me, I had to be better than my dad, and I had to stay there for my children when and if I ever became a dad. Following that incident, I began to ask questions about my dad only to have my mom respond by saying I am your mother and your father, and don't ask me another question about your sorry ass father. He's not here and won't be coming through those doors anytime soon. I can still hear it today, and I am still a little angry that she wouldn't answer my questions. However, that didn't stop me from becoming a good father. The day little Madison was born, I made a pledge with God to stay and be the best father I could be, and not the father that she would have to lie about, make up weekend stories about, or the fictitious father that I had to live with all of my life.

Many men are just like my father, fictitious; fictitious in the way they run at the first sign of a child. No sooner than the woman utters the words I am pregnant does the fictitious dad find a ticket for the next plane to anywhere but there. He is the epitome of the runaway dad that travels about producing offspring that he has no intention of fathering. You see, anyone can be a dad; however, it takes a real man to be a father, a man that doesn't just put in the work in the bedroom, however, he also puts in his work in the world room, the room where everything important about life takes place, the room where your little one will need your guidance for the rest of his/her life

I hear men everyday talk about how relationships aren't fair and the children always choose the mother over the father. Well here's food for thought, maybe more men should join in on being the functioning parent that drives the minivan in the morning dropping off the vanpool students, or that guy that host the birthday party with 10 friends spending the night, and finally, the father that shows up on parent/teacher conference night to find out what's going on at your child's school and develop a working relationship with your student's teachers.

There's nothing wrong with being that guy, the guy that wants to be present in every aspect of your child's upbringing, the guy that listens to all the gossip and chimes in with common sense fatherly advice. Men I caution you, be that guy that wakes up in the morning to prepare a great breakfast while chatting with your youngster and going over their plan for the day. That guy that is present at recitals, sporting events, spelling bees, and anything else your little one wishes to conquer. Simply be there.

As fathers, we may never know the full impact of simply being there; however, you will come to realize how important it is for your child to see your smiling face as they run to kick that goal, or walk up to that podium to spell their word. My mom couldn't be there for my games, for as I stated previously I was raised in a single family household with a fictitious dad. However, even in a situation where the family has separated and a divorce has occurred, if both parents are about the betterment of their child, one of them needs to be there every time the child presents a situation where parental support is needed. And from where I sit, I made sure as the father, I was going to be there no matter what. There's nothing better than having your precious child run to you for comfort after either winning or losing a competition. In a moment like that, you come to realize just how important it is to be there for them, you realize just how important it is to be a father.

Oftentimes, my daughter would look up to see if her dad was in the stands for her game, or in the audience as she approached the podium to spell her next word, and just like clockwork, there I was loud and proud to be there for what I call some of the greatest moments of my life. If you've been missing out on your child's events and accomplishments, then this book is for you, it will guide you and give you advice for becoming a father, not just a dad because the moment you impregnated their mom you became a dad. Now it's time to make the next move in becoming a father, so when you take another look in the mirror, you will know for sure you have moved into the next level of parenting, you have become a father.

I am writing this book as a layperson, not as a Doctor, PhD, or any kind of subject matter expert, as they can be a bit deep for us. I wanted fathers of all backgrounds, ethnicities, and cultures to have a simple recipe for being successful as a parent. Whether you are married, divorced, widowed, or just a single dad, this book will have something for you as you have probably lived a life similar to mine. As I speak to other fathers, I am finding out that no matter what race, background, or area we come from, we all encounter the same challenges in raising our children, and then the question becomes should I stay or should I go. Never go, always stay, whether you have to divorce and live alone or something tragic happens, always choose to stay and become a father.

Now understand this men, when you stay, it won't be easy and anything worth fighting for usually isn't, however, this is a fight you've got to endure as your child's life hangs in the balance. Stay and complete your duties so your child will have the love that he/she deserves, the commitment from both parents to be there, and most of all, a strong man in their life that they can look up to and one day maybe marry or aspire to become. I wanted to be that man, so I chose to stay and endure, even when it felt like Madison hated me and wanted nothing to do with me, I chose to stay.

Believe me brothers; you will learn to be strong through enduring the many moments where your child will make you think that you are the worst person on the planet. Often times, over something so trivial you almost want to strangle them so they can't talk. You will be hated and thrown out with the bath water more often than not during the teen years; however, I told my children at that point, "You will hate me more than you love me, however in the end you will love me. I went on to say it might take until you are in your twenties before you truly love me; however, we will get there.

As their father, we must learn to be the parent, role model, leader, hero, and finally friend with the latter developing stronger as they age. It's definitely a process in which we were given no blueprint; however, in writing this book, I hope I am giving you a foundation and recipe for raising an exceptional child all while building a lifelong friendship. Through the good, the bad, and the ugly, I persevered knowing at all times my daughter needed me, she needed me to be the father God called me to be, and the father I signed up to be. Don't be fooled men in thinking that their mom is all they need, they need you as the father to be strong when necessary, and soft always, yeah I am still scratching my head too; however, we have to figure it out and stay...

I didn't write this book to say I am in no way a better father than anyone else, I wrote this book to give you insight on how I chose to be a father and some of the resources I chose during my transformation. It's not an easy job to take on; and yet so many of us go into as if it were. Hopefully, this book also falls into the hands of young men with thoughts of becoming fathers and serves as a caution. As I stated earlier, anyone can be a dad, but it takes a real man to be a father, I repeat, **a real man**.

The Future of Fathers will not transform you into a responsible father; however, it will give you insight and ideas for transforming yourself into the man you want to see when you look in that mirror. So as you begin reading; remember nothing here is personal; however, I am hoping it will challenge you, encourage you, and enlighten you.

Enjoy the read...

Chapter One
Getting /Being Prepared

Preparation is defined as: The action or process of making something ready or becoming ready for something. I would say that being prepared for becoming a father is of the utmost importance, and should be taken more serious than just about anything else you will ever do. We grow up being told we should go to school to prepare for life, we should go to church to become better individuals, and we should join the military so that we can fight for our country. It's frightening to me how no one ever says you should read this book, or talk to a child expert, or consult your physician, or pastor prior to having a child.

We are told to prepare for everything in life except parenting, and this is a subject that I truly believe is far more important than anything you will ever do throughout the course of your life. We as parents have to understand that raising our children is the most important, and yes I will repeat the most important job we will ever take on, for it will be our offspring that someday takes over the responsibility of managing this nation's economy, educating others, and nurturing the next generation that will follow in their footsteps. It's no easy task, but it's a task that we must take on and see through to fruition.

Getting prepared for fatherhood is vastly different than getting prepared for most other things in life, as you can't go out and hire a trainer or purchase a DIY manual to solve your problems. Preparing for fatherhood requires one to think outside the box, as there is no one way to harness this expertise, it is basically a learn by doing kind of trial by fire experience where I found mentors to be my greatest asset. Both male and female mentors can open your eyes to many of the dos and don'ts to childrearing; however, the road map to success is ever changing and challenging, so don't run at the first sign of failure, because you will have failures in becoming a father. The important thing is that you learn from these failures and keep on course for they will only make you stronger; and remember, strength is the key to surviving the struggles and becoming the fantastic father.

Preparation has to begin before conception, as prior to even beginning the festivities of pregnancy, we need to ask ourselves: Are we really ready for this? Because our lives are about to change drastically. That's right, hold your wife, partner, or significant other softly in your loving arms and ask the question: "Are we really ready to bring a child into this world?" If your answer is yes then you should agree that you will always work together towards the betterment of your child no matter what happens between the two of you, as this is a commitment that your child should be assured of, for he/she did not ask to be brought into this world. The two of you made that decision, and now that you have, it is of the utmost importance that you step up above and beyond all else to assure that your child will be given every opportunity to achieve success and become an integral asset to our great society.

My first daddy duties came way too early in life, as I was a 20-year- old youngster, yes that's right a 20-year- old youngster, and at age 20 we are still very young and naïve. So there I was trying to go to college, work, and become a dad all at the same time, which isn't the way to prepare at all as you will only be setting yourself up for failure. Don't be fooled into thinking you can add parenting to the list of all your many things, as becoming a parent will require your full attention if you are to truly be successful. Successful parenting requires you to give of yourself when there is nothing left to give, to be able to put others before yourself when you have your eyes on that new golf club, or car you've been wanting forever. Parenting is a lifestyle that once you sign up for it, you will need to put all else on the back burner in order to guide this new little person that you helped create, into a life filled with the most positive outcomes and precious moments they will ever witness. However, you must be there and you must be prepared.

So there I was 20 years of age and a dad, not a father, mind you, but a dad. I had no idea what to do next, however, I had enjoyed every aspect of conception, but now that my precious little girl was here, all I wanted to do was have more fun. Well I was greatly mistaken, because the fun would now be few, far and in between. We hadn't taken any parenting classes, I missed out on most of the Lamaze training, and we didn't seek out the advice of a single mentor. You see, what we had done here was set ourselves up for an eventual failure. That's right, and fail we did, as today my oldest daughter faces problems and hardships that if I had taken her upbringing more serious, they could've been completely avoided. However, I took the irresponsible route and my daughter ended up having to endure. Reason being, I just didn't prepare.

Here's my scenario, I got my girlfriend pregnant at 19, we moved into our own apartment, became a dad at 20, and never stopped partying long enough to figure it out. So there was this precious little girl starving for the attention and guidance of her irresponsible dad, and I was too busy paying attention to myself, my friends, and whatever else could draw the attention of my feeble little self. As I mentioned earlier, we might think we are ready and that we are mature enough to start a family at the age of 20; however, from experience, I beg to differ, and I will argue this belief with any level headed adult out there.

I took a look at statistics from 2002 on teen pregnancy and the numbers were startling. Nearly 750,000 teens became pregnant in the United States, which resulted in approximately 425,000 births, 215,000 abortions and 110,000 miscarriages. (a) More than 10% of teen births nationwide, numbering 50,000 in 2002, took place here in California. (a) Despite a steady decline since 1991, California still had the seventh highest teen pregnancy rate in the nation in 2000. Startling right? And these numbers are from the early 2000s. So where do you think they are today? I am afraid to ask, and I personally fell into this equation so I know once again through experience how difficult it is to try and raise a teen child. Come on now let's not fool ourselves, guys let's remain level-headed and use common sense when it comes to having children, let's take a long hard look in that mirror and ask ourselves: Am I ready? Am I ready to put someone else before myself? Am I ready to love someone unconditionally and spend all of my money, time, and energy nurturing someone more than I ever have before?

In 1995 I felt that I was ready again, and this time my wife and I got down on our knees and prayed to God this prayer: Heavenly Father we ask that you grant us this opportunity to have a child, and if You do we promise to give the child back to you and raise the child the right way honoring You in all things. We prayed this prayer because my wife was having trouble conceiving and had to have a couple of procedures done in order to increase our chances. Well, God answered our prayers and gave us a beautiful baby girl and we named her

Madison. What was different about this conception you ask, well first off we prepared, or should I say I prepared.

Yes, I prepared this time. I armed myself with the necessary tools to be a dad, a friend, and more than that, a father. I was in the picture from the beginning, my wife and I had talked about it, prayed about it, and sought out the influence of mentors that had gone before us. I talked, read, and sang to Madison while she was still a fetus; I woke up when my wife experienced morning sickness, and went to Lamaze and every prenatal appointment I could attend.

This was going to be the happiest time of my life, and I prepared my butt off. Then reality sunk in and I realized that even now with all this preparing, life still throws you curves and you have to roll with them and stay on course. Don't be fooled thinking that because you prepared that you won't encounter speed bumps, the good news is that you will be far more ready for them when they come along. All the preparation in the world won't ready you for all aspects of fatherhood; however, by being prepared, you will have a far greater chance of being successful and you will have equipped yourself with a father's mindset that will serve you far greater in the big scheme of things.

Parenting Expert Barack Levin suggests these five tips:

1. Your Free Time – Be ready, you will no longer have any.
Your time from now on will revolve around your baby. There are so many chores and tasks involved with a baby that you can simply forget about relaxing on the sofa and watching your favorite football game.
Instead of fighting it, simply accept the fact that from now on you need to dedicate your free time to the baby.

2. Patience – Being a good dad is all about patience.
A baby requires that you dedicate plenty of time for him, play with him, feed him, rock him on your hands, and sing to him and more. You cannot hurry a baby to finish his bottle of formula only because you do not have the time to be with him or force him to go to sleep instantly because you are late for something.
You need to be very patient with your child and with time you will see that your behavior contributed to his well-being and his normal development.

3. Schedule – Be prepared to lose control over your schedule.
If you were thinking that you will be able to squeeze some "baby time" into your schedule you were wrong, very wrong. There is no way that you can control his schedule especially in the first year; so instead, you need to have your schedule revolve around your baby's schedule. You will need to complete your tasks when he is asleep or when he is with your wife or relatives.

4. Efficiency – Because you have no more free time and you do not control your schedule, it means that you have very little time for yourself.
You need to learn how to become efficient with your time. Try to make lists so that when you have some free time, you can accomplish as many things as possible. When you care for the baby, try to also be efficient and productive to shave a few minutes here and there to help you cope with your daily routine.

5. Help Your Wife – Whether you like it or not, your wife will probably choose to be in charge of many baby related things.
You might agree and you might not but the most important thing here is help her with the baby feed, change, put to sleep, and play with the baby without offering or being asked to. Suggest helping

with the house chores, shopping, cleaning and cooking. Your wife is going through some rough times and she needs your help and support more than ever.

Remember the world is always changing

"It is much easier to become a father than to be one," wrote author Kent Nerburn/. It's true. Even for men who really want the job, it feels intimidating. We can master a sport or a career. But it's hard to control much of anything in fatherhood. When our baby starts wailing, we can't make him stop. When our son starts failing algebra, we can't make him pass. Fatherhood is much slower work.

And what does it mean to be a father today? Today's "traditional" family looks very different than in previous generations. The father's traditional roles of provider and protector have seen great change. Often, both parents work outside the home. The dangers we face are the more subtle and insidious attacks from a culture hostile to families. While we still have a need for a nurturing, care-giving mother inside the home, a father's traditional duties have undergone a transformation. His role as a provider has been split between parents. His role as a protector has grown less obvious.

Fathers today face a greater expectation to be far more engaged. With more moms pitching in as "providers," we expect dads to be better caregivers. We change diapers and cook and kiss boo-boos. And that's great. As fathers, we should rejoice in the fact that we can take a greater role in raising our kids. But men still feel wired a certain way, and often, modern fatherhood doesn't seem like it fits who we think we are. Yet God is always at work, pushing against our impulses and helping us grow ever closer to His plan. Our flesh and fears may try to slow us, but our Lord gives us a spirit of "power and love and self-control" (2 Timothy 1:7).

Chapter Two
Working on You...
The Man in the Mirror

Have you looked into the fathers' mirror lately? Tell me did you like what you saw? Because I know there was a point in my life when I couldn't even recognize the person I saw when I looked in the mirror. I knew it was time for a change, time for a human makeover, time for me to work on me. That's right, time to take on a new image, one of a real man, a man that will be there for his family and won't hesitate to put them before himself. That's what kind of man it takes to become a father, one that will go to the end of the earth for his family forsaking all else to assure their lifestyle and success. Are you ready to become that man? Because it takes hard work; and a willingness to change.

I must admit, it was difficult for me as I had never been married and wasn't at all okay with putting someone before myself. I know it seemed very selfish in which it was, however, all of those years of there being just me to take care of, just me to feed, just me to clothe, made it even harder to acquiesce. I had to pray about this one, and it wasn't easy at all because you never really realize how much you do for yourself until you have to do for someone else. I was selfish and it needed to change, it needed to change very fast. It was one of the toughest things ever for me to do, as all of my life I was able to purchase new clothes, go out to the clubs, go out on dates, and basically do my thing when I wanted to. Well now with my newly formed family, all of those things were about to come to a sudden halt.

I wasn't ready for this at all and I had to make major changes in my life to become ready, I had to work on me, I had to become a man, that's right a man, and if you think you are ready to become a father then you better be prepared to become a man because it's a prerequisite. There's no way you should step into fatherhood without becoming an adult man first, as only a real man should be allowed to sail these ever changing waters of fatherhood, for it is no easy task. My journey to becoming a man was arduous and the accountability that came with it had me taking long hard looks in that mirror wondering to myself would I ever get there.

There are so many parts to becoming a man, and now that I have braved the waters I'd like to share my journey on what it took for me to become the man I am today, the father to my two beautiful daughters Monique and Madison.

My story is that of someone that grew up with meager means; however, there was nothing that we ever needed that wasn't provided. Therefore, in my parenting today one will always hear me saying "You will always have what you need, however you may not always get what you want." I am sure my youngest daughter Madison will attest to that. With that said, working on me took quite some time, however I did finally get to the point where I felt like a man and I was now able to handle all of my own affairs, purchase automobiles, a home, and most things I wanted or needed to sustain my very own lifestyle. Then along came all those things that you grow up hearing about regarding the family, the minivan, and the house with the white picket fence. Well at 35-years-old when I stepped into this new lifestyle, I was a selfish little something, and I wasn't ready to be a father. The wife would nag day in and day out let's have a baby, we need to have a baby to solidify our family, and I want to have your child.

Well one day out of the clear blue, out of nowhere, I decided yep let's do it, let's have a baby and just like that we went to work. All during the process, I continued to work on me, I rededicated my life to Christ, I began to pray with my family, and I stopped all the going unless my family was by my side. At that point, it was usually my wife and I and my three stepchildren, as we were still putting the work in. The relationship with Christ is of the utmost importance, as it is your very foundation; it is where men find out how to truly become first a strong man of God, a reputable husband, and more than that, a father. I would never go into fatherhood without having a strong relationship with my Heavenly Father, it's just not fathomable. That relationship needs to be strong and the very foundation you ground your family on and I will speak to that a bit later.

So the work continued and speed bumps had to be endured, however, after dealing with some medical issues we were called into the doctor's office and given the good news. We were going to have a bundle of joy; it was at that moment I knew I needed to take the next step in working on me. I joined the gym to work on getting healthy so that I could be there for the long haul in being the best father I could be. I stopped eating out and began to prepare more meals for the family, and I took on more of the household chores. This was an easy one for me, as I am constantly cleaning so for my wife I was a major catch because she loved yard work and I love to clean the house, a win/win. However, I bring this up to say that as a man becoming a father, you will need to step up that part of your game as well, as sharing all responsibilities should become a part of your daily routine. We are working on the man in the mirror, remember?

It's not going to be easy, but it has to happen if we are to cross that finish line to fatherhood. Once there, you will see that it was all worth the rewards.

Working on you has to become your daily affirmation, as there will be times when the man in the mirror will look at you and say things like you can't do this, you don't have what it takes to be a father, or just go back to being selfish. It's easy to give up, but we all know anything easy is never worth fighting for. Don't give up, don't run out on the very thing that needs you most, your child, that beautiful wide-eyed bundle of joy that will someday grow up to make you proud, if you stay and fight that is. Stay and fight for the life you created, stay and fight for the family that you have come to be the head of, stay and fight for your life and you will never again doubt the man in the mirror.

Basketball great Kareem Abdul Jabbar suggests this twenty point plan to becoming a man:

Why should a young man listen to an old guy about the best way to become a man? Because the typical teen is not yet able to see a future past the next few months. That's not a fault of character, but the fact that teens' brains have not yet physically matured. The pre-fontal cortex (PFC) does not fully develop in most people until they're twenty-four years old. Yet, the PFC is responsible for regulating mood, attention span, impulse control, and the ability to plan ahead and understand the consequences of one's actions. In the meantime, it's up to the adults to guide them by showing the possible consequences—good and bad—of their behavior. With that in mind, here's his guide to becoming a man:

1. Learn who you are as an individual.

Figuring out who you are, what you care about, what you believe in, and what you stand for is the most important—and most difficult—challenge of becoming a man. We're all raised with people telling us what to think, how to act, and what to say. Sometimes those people are parents, teachers, ministers, and other so-called authorities. Sometimes they are our friends and peers. Most of the time, given the choice, we seek the easiest path, the path of least resistance. We go along to get along. Sometimes that's okay. But it's those instances when you opt for a different path that can really define you as an individual. The important thing is you make those decisions for yourself—not out of spite against authority figures, or because of peer pressure, or even out of fear of losing someone's affection—but out of conviction of who you are and who you want to be.

2. Stand up for yourself and your beliefs.

British statesman Edmund Burke once said, "The only thing necessary for the triumph of evil is for good men to do nothing." That's one of my favorite quotes because it reminds me that it's not enough to have lofty ideals and beliefs, you sometimes have to actually *get off the couch and defend those beliefs*. This is especially hard when you're hanging with your friends and they all express an opinion that is the opposite of yours. Because you're outnumbered, it's easy for them to ridicule your opinion. Be strong. Defend your opinions and beliefs. If you think it's wrong to be racist but someone in your group says something racist (or sexist, or ant-Semitic, or anti-gay), then tell them you don't agree and that you don't think they should make such statements. That's how these verbal bullies are eventually defeated. More important, you'll feel proud that you took a stand. Those moments you do nothing will haunt you for a long time.

3. Avoid a physical fight—if you can.

You're probably thinking, "That's easy for you to say, Kareem. You're 7'1" so nobody wants to mess with you." That wasn't always true. When I was a young boy, I was bullied. And my dad was a cop, so that made it even more embarrassing. Later in life, I took up martial arts and even trained with my good friend Bruce Lee. That's why you can trust me when I say that *fighting is almost always a mistake*. There's a Chinese proverb that says, "The man who throws the first punch has lost the argument." That means that when an argument turns into a fight, it's because the one starting the fight realizes he isn't smart enough to win verbally, so he resorts to violence. It's always the dumbest guy who resorts to violence.

What do you do if someone threatens you with violence? You walk away, even run away if necessary. Even if you're pretty sure you could take him. Bad things can happen in a fight, even if no one means them to. Someone can take an unexpected fall and crack his head open. Teeth can be knocked out. Facial bones can be cracked. And all the crying later about how "it was an accident!" won't change that.

So, if you're threatened, leave and tell your parents. Some people are of the belief that you should just go right after the bully, fighting him to show you're not afraid. While this works well in movies, it doesn't work as well in real life. These days violence tends to beget violence. The bully doesn't just slink away, he returns with a baseball bat—or worse. You can still stand up for yourself without resorting to violence: that's what Gandhi, Martin Luther King, Jr., Cesar Chavez, the Buddha, and Jesus did.

The only time you should fight is if there is no other recourse. You can't run, you can't talk your way out of it. If that's the case, hit first, either in the nose (sometimes the blood will discourage further fighting) or the crotch (because the pain will make it hard for him to chase you). One punch, and then run.

4. Play a team sport.

I'm all for individual sports—as I mentioned, I did martial arts for many years and also yoga. (Don't think it's a sport? Try it!) But playing on a team teaches you how to interact with others, adjust to various personalities, work together as a team, be generous, and many other character-building traits. The cool part is that you don't have to join an organized team; you can just go down to the playground or open gym and play pick-up basketball or volleyball.

5. Choose your friends for the right reasons.

Good friends can see you through a lot of the tough parts of growing up. But bad friends can actually be the cause some of those tough parts. Don't hang out with kids just to piss off your parents or try to be something that you're not. You waste a lot of your youth that way—and miss out of some meaningful friendships.

6. Fight your fear of the unknown.

We all have a tendency to hate what we don't understand, whether it comes in the form of different food, different cultures, or different ideas. There was a Yale study in which researchers examined the brains of people as they were presented with proof that an opinion they held was wrong. MRIs showed that when those people immediately rejected the new evidence, their brains released an addictive chemical that made them feel good. In that way our own bodies are actually encouraging our ignorance and fear. Fight that impulse. Becoming a man means growing, learning, and understanding—not cowering under a blanket with a handful of comforting notions.

(By the way, don't confuse physical bravery with intellectual bravery. It's easier to jump out of a plane—hopefully with a parachute—than it is to change your mind about an opinion. Acts of physical bravado will give you an initial rush, but exploring a new culture or examining a new idea will mature you and make you the kind of person others will be interested in.)

7. Listen to advice.

Whatever troubles and doubts you're facing, billions of guys before you have gone through the same thing. Your dad probably knows exactly how you feel most of the time because he can remember the same pain and anxiety. Listening to people's advice doesn't always mean taking it. You have to decide which advice is right for you. But it might be a good idea to collect some quotes from those who came before you so you can refer to them when you need to.

I'm going to get you started with one of my favorites from philosopher George Santayana: "Those who cannot remember the past are condemned to repeat it." That means that if you don't learn from the experiences of others and yourself, you will end up making the same mistakes over and over. So, when someone gives you advice, don't dismiss it just because they're older than you.

8. Be politically aware.

One clear difference between children and adults is an awareness of your community outside your circle of friends and family. The world is constantly changing. Whether it changes for the better or the worse depends on the actions of those willing to get involved. Kids who don't know anything about their world try to hide it by saying, "I don't really care. It doesn't affect me." But that just confirms that they wish to remain children and have adults tell them what to do and think. Part of being a man is to be informed so you are prepared to take an active and responsible place in your society. Read newspapers, magazines, watch the news. Discuss these subjects with your friends, but always while respecting each other's opinions.

9. Mind your manners.

When you're a kid being told to firmly shake hands, keep your elbows off the table, or ask guests if they'd like a drink, it all seems like a load of dumb and arbitrary rules. Some of it is. But part of becoming a man is the realization that it doesn't matter whether or not the rules of manners make sense. What matters is the effect of following these rules: people appreciate the effort and respect shown them. In turn, they will show you respect.

10. Be patient in love.

Most of the information boys have about girls is WRONG! WRONG! WRONG! It's based on stereotypes, rumors, bad songs, shallow teen movies, and immature celebrities in personal tailspins. The worst thing you can do in looking to find a significant other is to try to change yourself into something you're not just because you think that's what girls are looking for. It doesn't work.

The best way to get an idea of what's attractive to girls is to talk to them. Like a girl? Get to know her, ask her about herself, and then show her you've been listening to what she says. Did she mention a book she likes? Send her an article about the book. It's low-key, non-stalkerish, and shows you care what she talks about.

11. Stay fit.

It's hard for all those teenage boys with turbo-charged metabolisms to understand that their bodies will not always be evaporating the masses of greasy calories they consume. They can eat a pizza and a tub of ice cream, and then run three miles. They can't imagine that will ever change, even when you show them photos of their lean dads' as teens and they look at the potbellies that have miraculously appeared later. But eating somewhat healthily and maintaining an exercise regimen will not only help fight off diseases and aging, they'll also help ensure an active lifestyle for many years. In other words, the body is like any machine: It may run great when it's new, but after years of neglect it will slow down, and eventually break down. Then you're the one vegging on the sofa while your pals are playing pick-up ball at the gym.

12. Never, never do something on a dare.

"I dare you" may be the three most dangerous words in the language for kids. The challenge to prove yourself to others is very tempting, especially since the alternative seems to be showing yourself to be a coward. But that's not really the case. The person who dares you is counting on your not being strong or smart enough to see this challenge as the empty, laughable joke it is. The person who refuses a dare displays intelligence, courage, and independence. And that's what daring someone is trying to rob them of.

13. Get organized.

One main difference between a boy and a man is that boys talk about what they want to do and men actually do those things. Another difference is that men have less time to accomplish more. In order to do all the things they want, they have to be organized. They keep a calendar (the one in your smart phone is handy), they make a to-do list, and they don't put off doing things until later. Being organized can change your life: you do more things you want to do, you finish things you need to finish, and you have more time to pursue new activities and relationships. In general, you will be much more successful.

14. Find heroes to copy.

There are so many worthwhile people to look up to and try to emulate, people from history, even characters in books and movies. The trick is in picking the right people for the right reasons. Skip most sports, music, and movie/TV celebrities. It's not that they aren't nice people, but the fact that they're successful and make a lot of money doesn't make them wise. Often, it's just the opposite. They pursued fame and glory so single-mindedly that they have no other interests and minimal education. Many are woefully misinformed about current events, yet at the same time frequently offering their weak, misinformed opinions. Don't make the mistake of believing that just because a person can act or sing, he or she also has valuable insights into politics or culture. Find heroes—real or fictional—that embody the *values* that you want to have, not the bank account.

15. Be independent.

A man can take care of his own daily needs. In fact, he wants to. Make your bed, do your laundry, learn to cook, hang up your clothes. Slovenliness is the sign of an immature mind. The sooner you start doing things for yourself, the sooner you will have the respect of others—and of yourself.

16. Question authority.

Respect your elders but don't think them infallible. Teachers, parents, relatives, politicians, and well-meaning guys like me really do want what's best for you. But we aren't always right. Even when presenting supposed "facts," people can be misleading in an effort to manipulate you into being who they want you to be or doing what they want you to do. History is filled with politicians misrepresenting "facts" in order to convince the population to back rash policies. Teachers sometimes aren't caught up on the latest research. To be your own man, you will have to make up your own mind about things.

17. Get smart.

Making up your own mind doesn't mean "going with your gut," "listening to your heart," or any other such clichés, however. That's the lazy man's way of avoiding the work that comes with developing an informed opinion. Want to express an opinion about the election, the death penalty, or gay marriage? First, do your research. Don't rely on biased sources. Your goal is to find the truth, not just confirm an opinion you already held. Every time you express an uninformed opinion, others will dismiss you as a child, someone who can only parrot others' opinions. A man knows how to educate himself in pursuit of truth.

18. Express yourself.

Go ahead, dye your hair purple. Grow it long, shave it off. Wear all black, wear all white, wear boots, wear leather, and wear a dress. This is the time to try on new identities to see which ones fits you best. Sure, you might have to endure some taunts, but it's more important that you figure out who you are than caring what those shut-ins of the mind think.

(A word of caution: avoid doing anything permanent, like tattoos, because, just your taste in clothes, hair styles, music, and your thoughts about pretty much everything will change. What you think is really deep and insightful today will seem shallow and immature in a few years. And you don't want something you will later think is childish permanently etched on your body.)

19. Pay attention to the short run...

People who care about you are always talking about your future: what courses to take for your career, what sports will help you get into college, what to look for in the person you're going to marry. All that stuff is important to think about. But don't let planning for your future consume your present. Do some things just because they're fun now. Take that art appreciation class just because it would be fun to learn about it. Play *Injustice* just to see Wonder Woman kick Batman's ass. Read those Dead pool comic books just because they're wickedly funny.

20. ...But keep your eye on the long run.

Most of what's important to you now won't be in a few years. Friends will change. Priorities will shift. That can be a pretty scary prospect. Most boys are afraid of growing into their nightmare version of an adult: the flaccid, self-righteous, humorless sack of meat dumped on the couch shouting commands or barking advice that begins, *"When I was your age...."* Don't worry; it doesn't have to turn out that way. Another favorite quote of mine is from Thomas Jefferson: "Eternal vigilance is the price of liberty." He meant that the cost of freedom is to always be watching for someone wanting to take that freedom away, but a variation of that quote can apply here: "The price of being a man is eternal vigilance." Know who you are, what you stand for, watch for any assaults on your principles, but always be open to change if the evidence warrants it.

As I read through his suggested roadmap to manhood, I must say I was impressed as he put together some very good guidelines to live by, and to help develop young men into mature men that will have the ability to step into fatherhood and handle the position with poise and empowerment.

Again I will draw on my faith as I've done since becoming a real man, for it serves as a strong foundation and a key to being successful.

I Corinthians 16:13-14 tells us: Be watchful, stand firm in the faith, act like men, be strong. Let all that you do be done in love.

I Corinthians 13:11 tells us: When I was a child, I spoke like a child; I thought like a child, I reasoned like a child. When I became a man, I gave up childish ways.

God understood there would be challenges to becoming a man so He gave us direction, and He gave us time. Now as you just read, it's time to step up and become that man, the man that speaks to success, the man that when you look in the mirror is reflected as a father.

Chapter Three
The Common Sense Effect

Sense becoming a father, I've adopted a new look on life, and I call it my common sense approach. Throughout most of my life, like most folks, I've dealt with things on an emotional level and I found myself living a very stressful, drama-filled life. A life I like to say that was filled with strama (my word meaning stress and drama) so I took it upon myself to make a dramatic change. And I did, again adopting what I call the common sense approach. What did this approach do for me?

Well first and foremost, it got me to a place where I began to be more honest with myself and those around me, a place where I completely understood right from wrong, and most importantly, a place where I could develop a straightforward open relationship with my daughter. A relationship that today thrives because it is based on a common sense approach.

Webster tells us that common sense means: 1. the unreflective opinions of ordinary people. 2. Sound and prudent but often unsophisticated judgment. 3. The ability to think and behave in a reasonable way and to make good decisions. May sound a little uneducated right, well I beg to differ. Common sense is the very thing that puts one in a real life perspective, we know right from wrong, and common sense usually will tell you to do right. Folks have a tendency to shy away from common sense as it steers them into doing the right thing. Well when it comes to parenting, common sense is the only way. Don't go selling your child false hope and expectations, be upfront and honest and you will earn their respect eventually, and they too will soon understand the common sense approach. The sooner you begin to use common sense, the sooner you will see a development of a bond between you and your child. They need you to be honest, and common sense will breed that honesty because you will find out that with common sense, your child will come to an understanding that this is how we live, this is what we can and cannot afford.

Our children all grow up thinking we are the Bank of America, and that we can buy them whatever it is their little heart's desire. Truth be told, most of the time we go out of our way to prove them right; however, with that proof comes the reality that we have over extended ourselves making it happen.

Again, common sense would've told you I can't afford that and really shouldn't go into debt trying to. I used to tell my daughter you will always have what you need, but you won't always get what you want. That didn't sit very well with her at the time; however today, now that she has grown up a bit and is now attending college, she realizes exactly what I meant, and she understands just how much her father has truly done for her.

There was a time in our relationship when she wanted nothing to do with me because of what I call the Disneyland effect, a situation that usually happens within a divorce type setting. You know where one parent always tries to win the child over through buying things and letting them have everything their way, while the other has to serve as the disciplinarian and structured parent. Well I encountered the Disneyland effect for a couple of years where Madison refused to respect me or include me in anything that was going on in her life. A time when I spent many hours in tears feeling abandoned and alone, a time when I felt like I had done everything wrong. Well don't be fooled men, this is a time when you will need to stand firm in your beliefs knowing she is the child and is being influenced by outside sources vying for her love in all the wrong ways.

I mean it was like a two year experience, as during her junior and senior years of high school, she didn't invite me to any of her sporting events, performances, prom, or graduation. I basically had to stay on top of the school calendar in order to attend the events I wanted to witness. It was hard on both of us, as she was in the middle of a situation that she didn't choose to be in, because as parents we often create environments for our children that may not be the best; however, life sometimes dictates things where we lose sight of what's really important. I did that, I created a situation that hurt our family and put a wedge between myself and what really mattered, so now I had to deal with the consequences. We choose our behaviors, so we must deal with the consequences.

Had I been aware of my new found common sense approach, maybe the situation that caused my family to dismantle could've been avoided. The reality is, I hadn't become a man yet, so I ran head strong into another woman's arms, had an affair, and caused a rift in my marriage that couldn't be repaired. With that said, it doesn't give you the right to run away and shake the responsibilities to your child/children; it also doesn't give you the right to be angry. This is the time when you will need to regroup, put on your big boy pants and take on the responsibility of being there for your child continually and in every way. Look in that mirror and ask yourself: What would common sense tell you? What is the truth? If you have adopted this approach, then you will know what to do, and you will do the right thing, and be a father to your child above and beyond anything else that is going on.

Remember they didn't ask to be here, you brought them here and it is your responsibility to see them through to adulthood, just as your parents did for you. How could you now turn away from your child because your inability to adhere to the sanctity of your marriage? It's your duty to fulfill your responsibility, your duty to stay and step up. It's kind of like WWJD (What Would Jesus Do?) well I am thinking He would probably use common sense in most situations as this would guarantee more positive outcomes. Basically, it comes down to choices, and if you lean towards the common sense approach, you will find that your choices

have gotten much better and that you are probably more so than not, doing the right thing.
Let's examine what the Bible says about common sense:

Question: "What does the Bible say about common sense?"

Answer: Common sense is sound judgment in practical matters. In Proverbs 8:5 some translations speak of the need to develop "common sense," which other translations simply call "prudence" or "discretion." Biblically, common sense can be thought of as a combination of wisdom and discretion (Proverbs 3:21; 8:12–14). Wisdom is knowing what to do; discretion is knowing when and where to do it.

Part of being a fool is having no common sense or being "void of understanding," as the KJV puts it (Proverbs 7:7; 24:30). The book of Proverbs proclaims the benefits of gaining wisdom and also shows the folly of being a fool (Proverbs 13:16; 16:22; 26:11). Proverbs 3:13–14 says, "Blessed are those who find wisdom, those who gain understanding, for she is more profitable than silver and yields better returns than gold." Wisdom allows us to see life the way God does. When we seek God's perspective, we can make decisions based upon their eternal significance rather than selfish interest. When we choose to make decisions based on wisdom alone, we are exercising common sense.

The desire for instant gratification is the enemy of common sense. Many people have become ensnared in trouble and heartache because they rejected a wise path and sought instead a path of immediate satisfaction. Common sense is often developed by learning from the consequences of such poor choices—the school of hard knocks educates many. Everyone makes bad decisions at some point. The difference between the wise and the foolish is that one learns from his mistakes and the other keeps repeating them. Some people seem born with a more level head, while others learn from experience. Either way, wisdom and common sense should be continually pursued in order to experience the best God has for us (Proverbs 2:1–8).

There you have it, laid out exactly how you should see it. Common sense, we should continually pursue it in order to experience the best God has for us, in order to become the best man you can be, and finally, in order to step into fatherhood and be the best father you can be. Your work is not done, as fatherhood is not a sprint, it is a marathon and you must be willing to dig in and finish the race so when we are done, we can look in that mirror and say job well done. That's common sense for you...

Chapter Four
Can we talk?

Okay so let's get a little deep here, and really begin to examine where we are as men when it comes to being a father. Let's talk about all the lackluster performances being put in by men who have the nerve to call themselves dads, particularly all these men that walk around with their chest stuck out like they deserve a medal or something. Really, we need to stop fooling ourselves men, thinking that because we impregnated a beautiful woman we have hit manhood, when all we have actually done is put another fatherless child on this planet. You know you ran, and you know who you are. That's right, I am talking to you, and just so you know I used to be you. Yes sir that's right, I was the man sticking his chest out like I had done something special when all I had done was fail. I failed to step up and be responsible for my actions, believe me, I enjoyed every minute of the development stages; however, I failed greatly during the nurturing process.

Failure, many of us have faced it, fought through it, and come out on the other side; however, many of us are still mired deeply in it. Where are you today in regard to your parental responsibilities? Are you still failing and can use the help of a mentor? Or do you need to recommit yourself to Christ or your family? Here's the good news, it's never too late to tune in, turn around, and turn out. That's right, the beautiful thing about life is that it is forever forgiving, and we as a people are also forgiving. I am in no way about to stand here and judge anyone, for I have sinned and fallen short in more ways than one, and I needed forgiveness so I know what it feels like. Just come clean and admit to yourself first, then find someone you love and trust to be open and honest with, as sometimes if you can just get things off your chest and out into the open, change can and will happen. It's when you keep it all bottled in, you begin to drown and become depressed and feel as if there is no one there for you.

That's wrong, that's where all negative influences come from and we don't need to stay in a place like that for any length of time. We need to surround ourselves with loving, caring, positive people that will lift you up instead of tear you down. We have all heard the old adages "you are what you eat," and "association brings about assimilation," right, well it's true and I tell folks all of the time, if you eat hamburgers, you will be a hamburger, but if you eat caviar well you get it. Choose those that you bring into your life's circle wisely my friend, as we want to associate ourselves with winners, with folks that have been successful in life and that have stayed and stepped up to their responsibilities as heads of their families. Role models that you would want to emulate, that you can turn to for sound advice instead of foolish counsel from losers that have always left and continue to leave at every opportunity.

It's time to stop crying wolf and start paying attention to your actions as a man, be honest with yourself as you are no good to anyone as the imposter you are in your home today. It's gotten so bad that you don't even recognize the man in the mirror anymore. You have become this self-centered all about me individual, while those around you are desperately searching for the husband, protector, and father they thought they were getting when you fooled them into believing you would be there. You have failed those that mean the most by checking out at the most critical time in the voyage, a time when you should be stepping up and taking on the responsibilities as the head of your family, and as the husband and father God called you to be. Not the run at the first sign of a leak in the ship type of leader, but the kind that digs in, plants his feet, squares his shoulders, and holds his head up, and proclaims I am fighting for mine. I am fighting for my family, and I am fighting for the future of fathers.

That's right; I am challenging you in this chapter, challenging you to stop talking the talk and to begin walking the walk fellas. I am calling on all the pretenders, fakes, and phonies to draw a line in the sand and take back your manhood, take back your rights as the head, and stop allowing excuses to keep you as the tail. I was once told nothing good comes from near the tail except a whole lot of bullshit, and now having lived a bit I concur. Men, it is time to stop falling for anything when we should be standing for what is right. Standing in the gap as promise keepers, men that pick up our crosses every day, and work towards keeping our promises, first our promise to our Heavenly Father, and finally our promises to our family. Keeping these promises should be the most important thing in your future, for if you are successful in keeping them, you will more than likely find that you have been successful in most of your life's endeavors.

I know it seems daunting, and for the most part it is, however, we put ourselves in this situation by lying in a bed that we probably were not prepared to lie in. That's right, hindsight is definitely 20/20 and if we take a look back, we will see that all we were was young, dumb, and full of cum. Not at all ready for fatherhood and definitely not ready for sex. Men we have got to stop allowing the little head to out think the big head, or the end to the fatherless child will never happen. We need to at least learn to wear protection, not only to serve as STD prevention, however to also serve as I am not ready for a child protection. Let's be real here, not too many of us were ready to be parents the first time it happened, and even sometimes when we think we are ready, we're really not. As I stated previously, a certain level of preparation has to take place, as even with preparation, speed bumps will be encountered, strama (stress& drama) will kick in, and the urge to run will heighten with each passing day.

Be strong men and remember you have what it takes today, yesterday you might've been that weak, put your tail between your legs and run dude, well today you are the man in the mirror that has decided to stay and fight. That's right; today you are going to make the choice to be the husband, to be the provider, to be the father you were called to be. Running is not an option anymore, as you are reading this book and should have no more excuses. I am not saying that by reading this book everything is going to be perfect, but what I am saying is that after reading this book you should have a much better attitude towards being a father and a new found will to finish this marathon called fatherhood. So don't stop here, for this is your first test, have the courage to finish reading this and you will have jumped the first hurdle. Put this down and you will probably never finish anything in life, for you will have proved to yourself that you haven't the ability to change. You will remain the guy I once was, the coward that uses alcohol and drugs to hide the real scars from running and hiding when the pressure got too high.

That's right, I called you a coward; however, you can change that opinion and that's the greatest thing about this life. We can reinvent ourselves time and again, however we can't take back time as it is a commodity we should hold very valuable, and if we are fathers it should be spent with our children loving, nurturing, educating, and inspiring them every step of the way. Fellas, we don't need another coward, I am tired of excuses and you should all be as well. Many of our dads were cowards, and it served us in no good way as there are thousands of men out there that continue to cower and leave a trail of fatherless children that don't deserve to come into this world without a father to support them and be that positive male role model that's needed in every child's life. Mothers shouldn't have to call big brother or big sister to serve in your stead; it needs to be you on the sidelines at the sporting events, you at the spelling bees and milestone events. That's right, it 100% needs to be you.

Stop confusing fatherhood with faking and show up for these events, don't just make empty promises and give false hope men, be the father that all the men aspire to be and that all the women wished they had married. Win that award and you will have earned your badge, you will have earned the right to stand in front of the fatherhood mirror and see what a true father's reflection looks like. So what's it going to be guys' courage or coward? Let's examine the two:

Merriam Webster defines Courage as: mental or moral strength to venture, persevere, and withstand danger, fear, or difficulty.

I ask: Do you have courage? Can you mentally and morally sustain the strength to withstand the fear and difficulties of life? It's not easy and I will not lie to you. Just having the courage to maintain your personal life is tough enough, as there's been many times when I myself wanted to give up and throw in the towel prior to even having a child. Then I had the courage or stupidity to add a couple of children to that equation which created more fear and stress. So if you think you are ready and that you have the courage, I caution you here to sit back and query yourself thoroughly for it is no easy task, especially in today's society. Seriously, I caution you, for I've made this journey and it is no easy trek. Sure I came out on the other side; however, I have many war wounds to show for it, and I would never tell you here nor in private that it didn't hurt sometimes, and that on many occasions I felt alone and unloved.

You will endure, as that's our mortal instinct, survival at any cost, especially when it comes to being there for your children. We have to become familiar with the big picture; our children need us in more ways than we could know. Our sons should want to emulate us, and our daughters should want to find a husband one day that is a man made in her father's image, that is to say if we are representing ourselves in a positive light. We should really be cognizant of our actions as parents, as our precious little ones are tuning in, and believe you me they will one day either follow in your footsteps, or let you know how bad of a father you really were, and it will hurt deeply, and that scar will never heal.

Find that courage fathers and become that man that's able to put his family first, whether it's a complete family, or a single dad, make the sacrifice and choose the betterment of your family over the selfishness you displayed as a child. The Bible says in I Corinthians 13:11: When I was a child, I talked like a child, I thought like a child, and I reasoned like a child. When I became a man, I put the ways of a child behind me. Have you taken that next step? Have you gained the courage to be a man that puts down childish things? It's not easy as we love our toys, however it is necessary if we are to be successful as fathers.

Now let's take a look at what Merriam Webster says a coward will see when he takes a look in the mirror. **Coward: one who shows disgraceful fear or timidity, a lack of courage or resolution.**

There we have it, plain and simple. Mrs. Webster nailed it, if you are a coward you are useless, you have no courage or resolve. You can't and probably won't finish anything in life, you are basically a loser. You will never be a father, but you have more than likely been a dad on more than one occasion, which means you are a part of the problem as you gallivant through life, leaving your seed in gardens; however, never staying around long enough to nurture or appreciate the beautiful fruit of your non-committal ways.

With my first child, I was that guy, I was you walking around with my chest poked out like I was the bell of the ball when all I really was, was a big loser, an irresponsible, selfish loser who puts no one before himself. Not even my child for God's sake, and that is a sign of immaturity, which surely meant I wasn't ready. Pay attention here, because I am going to give you a nugget. There's nothing wrong with being selfish, no one will ever hate you for being selfish; however, to bring children into this world and not have the courage to stay and be a father because you are selfish is just wrong. There is no place in this world for men like that, and if you know you are selfish and can't put others before yourself, then you should never, and

I repeat never become a parent. Who am I to say that, I am the offspring of a single mother that gave her all to do the best she could for all six of us; however, it wasn't enough because we deserved to have a father. I will not sit here and complain, because my mother was awesome; however, she cannot give the nurturing of a father, the leadership that children need from a man's perspective. The coaching and mentoring that only the father can pass down to his sons that will one day aspire to become fathers in their own right.

Crossing the line of parenthood is not for cowards, it's for men that can deal with adversity and turn it into advancement, that can take on obstacles and become stronger because of them, not cower and run at the first sign of them. If you are going to run, put on your marathon shoes and run into fatherhood, run into your responsibilities, and take on the challenge with a winner's attitude, and you will see, it may take a little blood, sweat, and tears; however, your reward will be worth it. The knowing that you stayed and became a father and that your children love and respect you will be something that no one will ever be able to take from you. You have to know that there is nothing like having your child say to you, "Dad I love you so much for being such a great father, and I hope that I can someday find a man just like you."

I am here to tell you that day was one of the best days of my life, that's right, the day Madison and I came back together and she hugged me and said she was sorry for things she had said and done. That was the day that I knew I had persevered above and beyond all the nastiness and bad days of feeling alone and hated. Yes, there will be those days because you made the decision to be a complete parent which means there's been days of discipline, arguments, and hatred; however, they will always be outnumbered by the days of love, togetherness, and family, that is, if you stay and finish the race. Remember, staying could look many different ways, however no matter what your staying looks like, happily married, divorced, widowed, or time spent separated, we must stay in the lives of our children, and not just stay; however, stay and be an active part of the parenting process.

Now that you understand that staying will be tough, you will need to begin to work on you. You must learn to possess strength in the face of adversity, courage in the face of peril, and the willingness to stand up for fatherhood no matter what the cost. You must learn to fight for the future of fathers so that those that come behind you will have men like you and I standing there holding that door open with a willingness to mentor and give advice when needed. Do not let the fear that you are feeling, breed failure, instead, plant your feet and square your shoulders, hold your head up and depend on God. That's right; again I say keep your head to the sky for that is where all good things flow from. If fear is present, then kill it with faith.

Four steps to overcoming fear:

First, be willing to take a risk. Yes, you might be hurt or embarrassed—so what? To overcome insecurity and gain confidence, you must allow yourself the freedom to take a chance. Start writing that book, take those music lessons, stand up and speak at the meeting! Feel the fear and do it anyway! "Fear of man will prove to be a snare, but whoever trusts in the Lord is kept safe" (Pr 29:25 NIV).

 Second, learn to laugh at yourself. Get over your obsessive need for approval and acceptance and learn to laugh at your mistakes. We're all human; stop taking yourself so seriously! When you make a mistake, be the first to see the funny side, and you'll find that people are more supportive than you think.

Third, start thinking realistically. It's time to drop the security blanket and realize it's not all about you. You are not the center of the universe, and your little faux pas don't mean that much in the bigger scheme of things. Besides, mistakes are often better teachers than success.

Fourth, reward yourself for little victories. When you complete a project, reward yourself. When you take advice or correction without retaliating, reward yourself. Often the people we lash out at are those trying the hardest to help us. Get used to the idea that you're valuable, talented, and skilled, and your worth in God's eyes is inestimable. Stop scrutinizing yourself through distorted lenses and start seeing yourself with 20/20 vision. Once you can do that, your fears will be replaced by confidence in yourself and in your future.

Chapter Five

They Need You There

Ask yourself this question. Did you need anyone there for you when you were a child growing up developing your senses and maturity? Well what was your answer? I am thinking your answer was yes, and if you answered otherwise you are a liar, that's correct, a straight up liar. We all needed someone and we all had someone, who that someone was is the big question. Tell me did you have a two parent household? I had a single parent household where there were five of my real siblings and two cousins all living with my mom. My dad was that guy they sing about in the song, "Papa was a Rolling Stone, wherever he laid his hat was his home and when he died all he left me was alone." Many of us were left alone and abandoned by our dads. I thank God for strong moms like the one that was in my household. I wouldn't be here today if not for Ms. Jessie Mae whom provided us with such amazing care that often times we didn't even miss a dad.

However, the reality is, we all need our fathers to be there, as a mother can never teach you to be a complete man, or could never be the father figure hero type dad all youngsters need to have in their lives. Yes, men they need us there in more ways than you could imagine, and if you look back on your life, those of us that didn't have dads, you probably felt the same way I did at times, mom doesn't understand me, my father didn't love me, I have no male role model or, no one to teach me how to be a man. I am sure there were times when you needed a man's advice and didn't have anywhere to turn to for it. Or as a female when you were thinking about dating and your mom just couldn't answer all the questions and you had to learn by doing, and yes, just like that, along came your first child.

Well, guess what men? If you were there; and he/she didn't have to do it alone, or without their dad, things could've been different and the outcomes more positive. Being there is one of the most important jobs we have as fathers, and it is a job we shouldn't take lightly, as a matter of fact, it is the utmost important job you will ever have. So before you decide to father a child, you need to decide to be there, and not only be there but stay there as a father no matter what. This is your responsibility, and you will need to man up and take it on. Your child needs a father, plain and simple. They need a strong male role model, a provider, a protector, a shoulder to cry on, and a father to wipe the tears and say everything is going to be alright. They need you there to pray beside them at night, and to see them off each morning as they embark on this crazy thing called life.

Especially in today's society, it is not a commendable thing to do, leave your children behind because you hate their mom or couldn't get along with her side of the family. Why should the children be made to suffer because the adults can't get along? Is it their fault? Did they ask to be brought into your mess? No they didn't, so if you stepped up to fatherhood to fail your child, I beg you please don't do it, as we don't need another fatherless child, what we need are heroes that will finish the fight for fatherhood.

Come on man, you know how it feels, your father failed you, and now you have the nerve to put that on your child because you are angry. Grow up man, you have persevered and you should feel good about it, you should've learned enough by going through your own pain that no child deserves to grow up without a father. You know better, and if you don't, you should know better now as you have been given some sound advice and excellent guidance on how to hang in and fight for the future of your child. Don't you dare put your tail between your legs and run out on your child, they need you. Dad, can't you see it in their little eyes? They need a father to be there in ways that no one else can, they need the strong arms of daddy to hold them when they fear, or the strong voice of daddy to scold them when they lose their way. Run and the negative possibilities will be endless; however, be there and you will be able to help them persevere in this life with many positive outcomes and successes. Being there is a requirement of fatherhood, and if you have no intention of being there, then why would you even venture into this? You are the worst kind of man for the job, and should look into the mirror and be honest. You should tell yourself, I am not father material and there's nothing wrong with that.

You are still a man. As a matter of fact, you are a great man, as you can be honest with yourself and those around you. I respect that totally, a man that knows he doesn't want children. Now all you have to do is find a woman with the same feelings and the world will be a perfect place. Having children is not some written or unwritten rule that states because you get married you have to become parents. Not at all, having children is a commitment, a commitment to God, one another, and to your unborn child, so if you can't be committed, do not have children because they will 100% need for you to be there. No matter what the situation, you will need to step up and be there, there is no choice about it, if you decide to become a parent, then be there for your child, plain and simply be there. There is no room for excuses here, this world has too many fatherless babies already, so if after reading this book you feel the need is there to become a parent, we as a nation don't want to hear any excuses, and we definitely don't want to have to fund your endeavors.

That's correct, when you leave and shirk your responsibilities as a father, we the taxpayers take the hit while you walk around bragging about another notch on your belt. Well guess what Mr. Man? Bragging is useless, as you are nothing more than a loser, a failure as a father, and meaningless as a man. Harsh reality, isn't it? Well just think of all the young fatherless children and what they have to deal with, now ask yourself: Is it tougher on them or you?

Why kids need their dads – Parenting.com

Four decades of research and hundreds of studies have proven what should be obvious to all of us: The more involved a dad is, the more successful his children will be. A father's influence can determine a child's social life, grades at school, and future achievements. Involved dads = Successful children. The dad effect starts as early as birth. A review of studies by the Father Involvement Research

Alliance shows that babies with more involved fathers are more likely to be emotionally secure, confident in new situations, and eager to explore their surroundings. As they grow, they are more sociable. Toddlers with involved fathers are better problem-solvers and have higher IQs by age three. They are more ready to start school and can deal with the stress of being away from home all day better than children with less involved fathers.

At school, children of involved fathers do better academically. For example, a study by the U.S. Department of Education found that children of highly involved fathers were 43 percent more likely than other children to earn mostly A's and 33 percent less likely to repeat a grade. They are also less likely to have behavior problems at school and to experience depression.

According to the Father Involvement Research Alliance review, girls with involved fathers have higher self-esteem, and teenage girls who are close to their dads are less likely to become pregnant. Boys show less aggression, less impulsivity, and more self-direction. As young adults, children of involved fathers are more likely to achieve higher levels of education, find success in their careers, have higher levels of self-acceptance, and experience psychological well-being. Adults who had involved fathers are more likely to be tolerant and understanding, have supportive social networks made up of close friends, and have long-term successful marriages.

Everyday activities are important

A study by Brigham Young University researchers finds that involvement in everyday activities, such as eating dinner together, watching TV, playing in the yard, and playing video games are even more important to share with Dad than big outings or trips, although those contribute to children's development as well. Fathers and youths in the study experienced more satisfaction and cohesion in their family when fathers were involved in everyday core activities.

"Although participation in balance family leisure activities is important and needed, it was fathers' involvement in the everyday, home-based, common family leisure activities that held more weight than the large, extravagant, out-of-the-ordinary types of activities when examining family functioning," the authors said.

Different approaches

But how does a father's influence differ from a mother's? Isn't one good parent enough? "Fathers and mothers have unique and complementary roles in the home," says Brett Copeland, a clinical psychologist in Tacoma, Washington. "Fathers encourage competition, independence, and achievement. Mothers encourage equity, security, and collaboration."
W. Bradford Wilcox, director of the National Marriage Project and associate professor of sociology at the University of Virginia, says that fathers' special input differs from mothers' in at least four ways: playing, encouraging risk, protecting and disciplining.

Playing

By asking parents of 390 families how they play with their children, psychologist Ross Parke found that "in infants and toddlers, fathers' hallmark style of interaction is physical play that is characterized by arousal, excitement, and unpredictability." Mothers, on the other hand, were "more modulated and less arousing" in their play. This became glaringly obvious to me when my husband left home for a year and a half to work in Afghanistan. My modulated play was not cutting it. Several months into the experience, our three kids began complaining to me, "You never tickle us." I had to take a page from my husband's playbook for a while.

A manual from the U.S. Children's Bureau explains the impact of fathers' play this way: "From these interactions, children learn how to regulate their feelings and behavior. Roughhousing with dad, for example, can teach children how to deal with aggressive impulses and physical contact without losing control of their emotions."

Encouraging risk

Where mothers tend to worry about their children's safety and well-being, fathers encourage their children to take risks. Psychologist Daniel Paquette's review of scholarly research found that dads are more likely to encourage their children to overcome obstacles, to talk to strangers, and to go in the deep end during swim lessons. One study in the review (J. Le Camus, "Les interaction pere-enfant en milieu aquatique") focused on a group of parents teaching their children how to swim. It found that "fathers tend to stand behind their children so the children face their social environment, whereas mothers tend to position themselves in front of their children, seeking to establish visual contact with the children."

Protecting

Perhaps it's their size, strength, or inclination to protect, but fathers appear to be better at keeping predators and bad influences from harming their children. Psychologist Rob Palkovitz said in The Atlantic, "Paternal absence has been cited by multiple scholars as the single greatest risk factor in teen pregnancy for girls." When fathers are more involved, they can better monitor what's going on in their children's lives, including interaction with peers and adults.

Disciplining

Although mothers discipline more often, fathers discipline with a firmer hand. In their book Partnership Parenting, Drs. Kyle Pruett and Marsha Kline Pruett write, "Fathers tend to be more willing than mothers to confront their children and enforce discipline, leaving their children with the impression that they In fact have more authority." Mothers, on the other hand, try to reason with their children and rely on kids' emotional attachment to them to influence their behavior. Although Mom and Dad may not seem to be on the same page, this diverse approach can be very effective in disciplining children.

The good news about being a dad is that you don't have to be spectacular at it to make a major positive contribution to your child's life. W. Bradford Wilcox looked at data on delinquency, pregnancy, and depression in adolescents and compared the statistics with how the teens rated their fathers or if they lived with a single mother. He found that outcomes for teens in single-mother homes were about the same as those living with both a mother and a poor-quality father; teens had higher levels of delinquency, pregnancy, and depression. But teens living with their mother and father, with whom they had an average-quality relationship, experienced much lower negative outcomes. Teens that had a high-quality relationship with their father had even lower rates.

Wilcox concludes that "great, and even good-enough dads, appear to make a real difference in their children's lives."

Children Are Better Off With a Father Than Without One:

It can be tempting — in a world where women are increasingly likely to be single mothers, "breadwinner moms" or supermoms seemingly able to do it all — to think of men as superfluous to the family. From Hollywood to academia, this view has tremendous currency. In "Raising Boys Without Men," for instance, the Cornell psychologist Peggy Drexler put it this way: "women possess the innate *mom power* that in itself is more than sufficient to raise fine sons."

But the view that men are superfluous in today's families is dead wrong. While it is certainly true that some children raised without fathers turn out just fine (I did), on average, girls and boys are much more likely to thrive when they have the benefit of a father's time, attention, discipline, and especially affection.

Boys are more likely to steer clear of trouble with the law when they grow up with their father in the home. One Princeton study found that boys raised apart from their fathers were two to three times more likely to end up in jail before they turned 30. Dads matter for daughters as well. Another study found that girls whose fathers disappeared before the girls turned six were about five times more likely to end up pregnant as teenagers than their peers raised with their fathers in the home.

And we know that kids — especially boys — are more likely to excel in school, and to steer clear of the principal's office, when they are raised in a home with a father who takes their homework and school conduct seriously.
So, even though many men cannot or need not serve as the primary breadwinners in their families, modern couples need to recognize that fathers' contributions to their children's welfare extend well beyond money.

President Obama put it well: "Of all the rocks upon which we build our lives, we are reminded … that family is the most important. And we are called to recognize and honor how critical every father is to that foundation. They are teachers and coaches. They are mentors and role models. They are examples of success and the men who constantly push us toward it."

I didn't want to write this chapter with just the dissertation of a proud father that stayed through much adversity; I wanted to add substance from highly educated professionals that speak to the importance of the much needed father's influence in the rearing of our children. I wanted you to know that this is a real world issue, and I need you to know that you are integral to your child's future and if you don't stand up and take on your role, your child will likely fail in life.

Look men, I am always going to keep it real with you, I too was once a failure as a father, I wouldn't be able to sit here and talk to you about fatherhood had I not looked in that mirror and said to myself, "You will change, you will stop putting yourself before others just to attain self-gratification. I learned the hard way guys, and now I want to give all men the opportunity to use a mulligan if you will. What's a mulligan you ask? In golf the term mulligan means you get a second chance, and with that second chance comes the opportunity to change what is wrong and make it right. It is an opportunity to refocus and create in you a new man with a deeper love for life and the confidence to step up, and take command of the responsibilities placed before you.

And better yet, if you are reading and haven't quite begun your journey into fatherhood, you can now make sound judgments on whether or not it is time to even embark on such a journey. You can also use the tools that are being offered up to prepare yourself for fatherhood, and to gain confidence, maturity, and knowledge which are all very positive and strong characteristics of a successful father. A father that will endure the ebbs and flows of life through standing firm; and keeping your faith. A father that will not run at the first sign of tension and struggle; however, you will dig in and fight for your family.

Again let's examine what the Bible offers us:

Ephesians 6:4

Fathers, do not provoke your children to anger, but bring them up in the discipline and instruction of the Lord.

The Role of a Father:

There is no role in our modern society that suffers greater neglect as far as God is concerned than that of the father. Not only has God given men the incredible privilege of imitating Him as Father, He has placed upon the shoulders of fathers an incredible responsibility. As our society has chosen Father's Day to celebrate fathers, it is appropriate to remind fathers of their God- given responsibilities.

Accountability

Children are a blessing from the Lord (cf. Psa. 127:3-5). As with all blessings, there is accountability. Fathers must realize that the Spirit gave this charge regarding our children to us. He did not give it to the mother, though their role is absolutely necessary in its being carried out. He did not give it to the daycare. He did not give it to the babysitter. He did not give it to the nanny. He did not give it to the grandparents. Nor did He give it to the church, the school, or the youth program. He gave it to fathers. Therefore, fathers will bear the accountability-the consequence for failing to carry it out, or the reward for so doing.

The reward will only come if you choose to stay, running away and cowering is the world we were raised in, and it was a vicious cycle. These cycles were meant to be broken, as I lived through this cycle and I've dedicated my life to defeating it wherever it is present. Maybe your home couldn't break it, but you can by choosing to stay and becoming a father. By earning the badge of fatherhood and sending out into this world well-educated, God-fearing young adults that will honor and respect God, family, their community, and nation.

Chapter Six
Have No Fear

With fatherhood comes many fears, mostly the fear of failing, as many of us come from households where our father failed to step up to his responsibilities. I say to you, destroy that rearview mirror and refuse to let the failures of our fathers hinder you, or have any adverse effect on your success as a father. Again, things can only be cyclical if we allow them to be; however, if we decide to be the men God called us to be, fear should have no place in our lives. Of course it's not that easy, as I still struggle at times with fear myself; however, you won't beat that fear unless you move forward into it and come out victorious on the other side.

Fear will only remain when there is no effort put forth to challenge it. I always say you will never know if you don't try, and trying takes effort. Basically, our dads lacked effort, and if we continue to walk in their footsteps, there will be no change. I allowed fear to win in my first attempt at being a father; however, I was a child then and by the grace of God, I was given a second chance, and fear could not keep me away from being the best possible father I could be to Madison. Again, I caution you here young men, as I just reiterated how important it is to be a man in raising a child, as life has no place for children raising children. This is no game, as life itself presents fear of the unknown, now you want to bring parenting into the equation as a young child, not recommended. I am here to tell you my friend, you are not ready, and no child should be forced into a world of uncertainty because you thought you were.

As a young father, I was not prepared for the fear that came along with being a parent, as one needs to be both mentally and physically prepared for such an adversary like fear. It is not for the weak and feeble as it comes in many different forms and measures. There's the fear of what your child knows and what they've been told by others that can lead to the demise of every good thing you've tried to implement. These things alone can create a wedge between your child and yourself that can take years to repair, and that will take years off your life. But again you will have to endure as this season will pass if you plant your fatherly feet and refuse to run. Why run? I didn't. I looked my daughter in the face and said, yes daddy did those things; however, he didn't do them you, did he, and one day you will have your life in which I will not ever judge you for your actions, nor your faults. It's simply not their business, and if you've been there as a father, don't allow them to punish you for how you lived, or hold over your head things that they may have heard from an angry mom or relative. If you do, you have allowed fear and the mind games that will be played to push a weak man away from his responsibilities as a father.

That's right; your child is going to instill fear into your heart. They will use what they are given to put you into a state of fear where things you don't want them to know might have to come out. I say this, let the skeletons out, and show your child that no matter what they think they know, or how much they hate you for what they think they know you are going nowhere and they will respect and love you even more once you've gotten through this impasse. I had no intentions of ever sharing the negativity of my past with my daughter; however, when divorces occur and the nastiness and hate begins, you won't be able to control the outside voices, and believe me, there will be outside voices; however, you will be able to stand firm and look that fear in the eyes by owning up to the truth and setting the record straight.

Remember your child is not raising you, so if and when they try to judge you, speak firmly to the issue, allow room for communication, but in no way apologize for the life you have lived. It's simply not there business.

Then there's the fear of not being able to afford everything your child might want, which means going through the I hate you dad, and the I wish I was born into a different family syndrome. Well men, I have always stood firm in letting my child know that she will always get what is needed; however, you may not necessarily be receiving everything that you want. Again, you can turn and run because you fear your child hates you, heck if you are raising them the correct way, they are going to hate you most of the time. I continually found my resolve in knowing that they will absolutely love me in the future, once they are able to realize the life that was given to them, and how much you really loved and cared for them. Children are always going to want everything they see their friends getting; however, reality says this is what we can afford, and this is how we live.

Do not allow yourself to get caught up into the trap of keeping up with the Joneses, because with that comes even a bigger fear, the fear of being mired in bills that never should've occurred. Being over your head in bills is another reason for fathers to run, as we become embarrassed by a mindset of thinking we just aren't good enough and our children won't love us. Bullshit, you have to learn first of all that this is the hand that you were dealt and what needs to happen is that as the head of your household, you need to take the reins and let your family know this is how we live, and by no means are you going to get in over your head. We can't all be millionaires, so kill that dream quick and continue to be that father that gives what is needed, and that assures their successes.

Fear can in no way be the obstacle that hinders your fatherly duties, instead let it be the fuel that gets you to the finish line of fatherhood. Let it be the force that drives you into the arms of your children, knowing that you have to be bigger, stronger, and smarter in order to persevere, for if you don't, as fathers, we have no future. Fear has taken its toll on enough men, and if you take a look around, there are enough cowards that are avoiding their responsibilities to their children. It's time to use that fear as a motivating factor in your life and not as a reason to push those in need of you away to avoid failing. You have to understand that failing is temporary; and that if you want to win, you must pick yourself up, dust yourself off, and get back in the fight. That's right, get back into the fight, as it is the fight of your life and if you fail, not only will you be failing as a father; however, your children will most likely fail at some point to survive this life as well.

Don't fear failure men as we all fail at some point in life, whether on a test, or in a relationship the one constant, is we keep on living. Failure won't kill you, and if you have heart, it should only be temporary as you will get back up, and kick failure in the ass. Just keep moving through, and moving past your failures; and you will see that life moves on and honestly, no one is even focusing on your failures. It's the victories that count, and the only way to beat a failure is to become victorious, and I guarantee you dad, if you stay, victory will be at hand. You won't fail, you can't fail, if you stay and fight no matter what the outcome, at least your child will have witnessed a father that displayed the relentless will to do the right thing facing all adversity. And as a father, you will have instilled in your child the will of a fighter with a passion to succeed.

Speaking of relationship failure, how about the fear that comes after a divorce takes place and you become the non-custodial parent. Man this can get ugly real fast, for if your child has heard the heated arguments and witnessed you and mom going at it, choices could very well have already been made, and you might not be their choice, as loyalties are usually made towards mothers. Especially in the case where your child is a female, she will almost always side with mom. This alone will create in you a fear that many men just don't survive. With all the bitterness the divorce has summoned, you now have a daughter that basically wants to divorce you as well. Your first thought, to hell with it, let her and her mom both go as my life will be better off. Well not so fast my friend, that's what I call the escape clause, when actually it's a fear of losing your daughter. Its automatic men, your daughter is going to want her mom as they hold the same image and thought process; however, you can't let fear win.

Your daughter loves you, and she needs to know you love her above and beyond all that is going on. She needs to see that you are not going anywhere when it comes to her, and that you plan to take on every part of your fatherly duties. What happened between you and her mom, once again is simply not her business, so you need to step up, speak honestly to the issues and let her know dad isn't divorcing you, you are my responsibility. However, your mom and I will no longer be married, and that should in no way change how either of us cares for you. Communication is vital here, and if you fail to communicate properly and with authority, you will lose your precious little girl. You can't lose dad, it's not a choice, and your daughter needs you now more than ever. Would you really like to see some other man stepping in and taking on your fatherly responsibilities? Do you really want to be that guy that misses out on every aspect of watching your little girl transform into a beautiful woman? Let fear win and that's exactly what you will become, your daughter's biggest nightmare, a father that failed her.

I speak mostly to daughters here, as most sons go with the flow and usually the father/son relationship isn't stymied due to the many things they might have in common. However, often times a bond is forged between a mother and son that could prove to be just as tough for a divorcing father; however, once again, you must dig in and let everyone involved know that this father will be a part of the big picture, and that he will be an active parent in all the decision making.

You see, even with all the fear and uncertainty this world can bring, it all boils down to how much you as a man are willing to endure to make absolute sure that the children you bring into this world will get that fighting chance, because you were able to look fear in the face and move beyond the wake of losers that have allowed it to take their rights to fatherhood as if they never existed. That weak-hearted coward that has not only allowed fear to hinder him, however he has allowed it to hinder his every offspring rendering them futureless and fatherless.

I urge you to take to heart your responsibilities to the children you bring into this great nation, and be there above and beyond the fear that comes with this life, for if you don't you will have added to the meaningless communities of cesspools where those with nothing feed off of the nation's working class, and show no enthusiasm or effort to change. Seriously think about it, do we need another fatherless child or single parent household where the mother struggles to keep a decent job and food on the table because you decided to be a deadbeat dad. Plain and simple, the answer is no, and I am challenging you as a man to defeat the fear. Don't let the murmuring, the voices in your head, the loss of a job, not having a car, or any of this temporary bullshit take you out. Choose to win man, choose to understand that we choose our behaviors and for that very reason we also choose our consequences. So when you choose to have sex with your soon to be baby momma, understand that you have chosen to deal with what consequence comes with that choice: Your child is your commitment for life, and you owe it to that child not to succumb to fear in any shape, form, or fashion.

Dr. Mary Lund had this to say about challenges fathers face after divorce:

A non-custodial divorced father faces many challenges in establishing a new relationship with his children after his marriage ends. During marriage, a father may fulfill his parenting role indirectly by supporting the mother's caretaking and by being the breadwinner. A father who divorces will probably become one of the 90 percent of men who do not get custody. (Richards and Dyson, 1982, Weitzman and Dixon, 1979).

In the aftermath of marital separation he may find emotional and practical obstacles to continuing a relationship with his children from a distance which require him to make more of a direct commitment to parenting than he did before the separation. As many as 50 percent of divorced fathers in the US and the UK do not overcome the challenges and have less than yearly contact with their children. (Fulton, 1979; Gingerbread and Families Need Fathers, 1982). However, many fathers do master the struggle and are rewarded by good relationships that benefit both the children and fathers.

You see even here she speaks to the percentages and the numbers are startling. We have got to master the struggles men, and not allow any type of obstacles the ability to take us out as not only your life depends on it; however, more importantly the life of your precious children hangs in the balance. So fear not my precious son, for our Heavenly Father will hold you in the palms of His hands and see you through to the finish line.

Biblical guidance regarding faith:

Isaiah 41:10 – Fear not, for I am with you; be not dismayed, for I am your God; I will strengthen you, I will help you, I will uphold you with my righteous right hand.

2 Timothy 1:7 – For God gave us a spirit not of fear but of power and love and self-control.

Psalms 34:4 – I sought the Lord, and he answered me and delivered me from <u>all fears.</u>

This is powerful, as the Psalmist states all fears, not just a few fears; however, all fears, so men of God pick up your cross and carry it into this life without fear, for our Heavenly Father has you right there in His righteous right hand.

Chapter Seven
Father or Friend

The subject of father vs. friend is a very touchy subject, as parenting is an art form and not a science, so evidence leaning either way is mostly that of trial and error. From my perspective, I will say that there are times when you will find yourself feeling like a very close friend; however, in a moment's time, your child will put you back into the real world where you will need to become that parent once again. For that reason, I've learned to keep my parenting face on most of the time when it comes to my relationship with Madison. It's almost like they lure you in with the friendship game just to get what it is they are trying to get out of you; however, the moment they are hit with fatherly resistance, you become the worst parent in the world. All of a sudden, just like that you are hated, all because as a friend you failed to do for them what they wanted and now like a friend that doesn't listen to the leader, you are banished. And believe me, you will be banished for quite some time, for as in friendships folks come and go depending on how much they are willing to give or bring to the table.

Look at some of your friendships: What was the foundation of some of them and how quick were you to banish friends when they didn't function according to your guidelines? Count how many of your so-called friends still remain true to you today, and how many, if any, can you still call on in the case of an emergency? Now ask yourself: Is that the kind of relationship you want with your child, where either of you might walk away because your feelings were hurt or you heard something about them that pissed you off? Well that's what you will be getting if you allow yourself to put friendship before parenting. Most friends are yes folks, and will say to you what you want to hear and usually if you are strong-willed they will also jump when you tell them to. Try being a friend to your child before being a parent and they will have you jumping through hoops faster than you can ask yourself who am I here.

I mean don't get me wrong here, there have been times when I introduced my daughter as my best friend; however, she was a bit older and understood the coalition. Not at any time while growing up did she ever think our relationship was based on a friendship type situation, for in order to lead her as a father, I could never allow her to think she was my friend. You have to know your child, and understand their mindset, for if they are strong-willed like Madison is, they will use the friendship situation to their advantage and you will be rendered helpless as a parent. I caution you here men, as it's hard enough being a father to your children in today's society with all the problems we face, now throw being a friend into the mix, you better watch out as you will be playing with fire for sure. Our children need us to be parents, as they will have many friends to butt heads with and battle for control.

They need to you to be that father that is in control and that will lead them through this crazy thing that we call life. Remember back when you were a kid and if you had a father in the house, I guarantee you he wasn't trying to be your friend, and if he was a strong leader, he spent more time tapping that ass than he did playing friendly games. I'm not saying we need to beat out children down; however, what I am saying is that we need to spend more quality time with them. You know, time working on building a positive relationship such as eating dinner at the table instead of everyone doing their own thing, or time assisting them with their homework, or other school projects. That's right dad, this is what you signed up for when you decided you were ready to become a father, spending meaningful, positive, productive time with those you are responsible for as a dad, and not a friend.

You have to understand the difference here, friends for the most part will come and go; however, a father has to be there for the long haul, and he must be willing to take the good, the bad, and the ugly. You see when things are going great and there's fun to be had, your friends are all over you, and there is barely room to breathe; however, let things take a turn for the worst and the fun is over, those so-called friends will be gone with the wind; however, a father will be there to pick up the pieces and put things back in order as a father should. Not take off like a fair- weathered friend that when the rains came, grabbed his umbrella and kept only himself dry. There is definitely a difference, and depending on the outcomes you would like to see, make your choice and learn to live with it; however, I will warn you, if it's friends you are looking for, don't look to your child for that relationship.

A parent/child relationship is far more different than a friendship, a friend can walk away at any given time; however, a parent, now that's a lifetime bond that comes with far more emotional baggage than any friendship ever could. I liken a father/child relationship to that of a marriage, as it comes with emotional roller-coasters, mental struggles, good and bad days, and sometimes someone wanting divorce. I mean honestly that's the reality of parenting, you are married to your child and for the most part a divorce can't happen so you are locked into figuring it out. Now as a friend you won't even care about figuring shit out. It would be easier to walk away and say I never really liked them anyway; however, as a parent that's not even a choice there is no walking away that is if you have decided to stay no matter what and be a father. However, if you are weak and only a friend, you can run and abandon your responsibilities, for as I stated earlier, that's what friends do. Are you getting it? Friends shirk promises and responsibilities just like that, as there are no true ties or commitment; however, a father he is committed for life, and should never flee his commitment to his children.

I want you to understand me here as I'm not saying you should never be a friend to your child; however, what I am saying is that early on, in my opinion, we should lean more towards being a parent as these are your child's formative years and could very well influence their entire future. These are the times when we should be nurturing, guiding, and parenting our children to assure they develop a relationship with Christ, a thirst for education, a life of diversity, and a willingness to give back to the very community in which they reside. If as parents we impact our children to live these types of lives, we will have created a generation of young men and women capable of moving mountains and becoming tomorrow's leaders that will have the ability to move forward this nation in a positive and empowering fashion. Then once we are through that, we become friends and stand together side by side in creating a better place for those that will follow.

Remember, your young child will have friends, and hopefully those friends will be as diverse as our nation, because that's what needs to be instilled into the youth of today. Diversity, we need to raise our children to know and understand that all people were created equal and that we should love everyone. There's enough racism in this world today, and if we as parents are going to do the right thing for our children, we should be teaching them to be as diverse as possible so that we can abolish these race wars and all the racial profiling that comes with it. You want to be a friend, then as your child grows up and develops his social mindset, be the friend that creates in them a friend to all mentality, then let them know that there is no line on the color bar, and that we are one people under God. Be a real friend when it comes to that time, and show them how to break through that color barrier that causes hate and division.

That's when you become a friend, when they become young adults and are being influenced by all the outside noises that might cause them to go astray, that's when you step up and become their best friend. The friend that teaches right from wrong, and that shows them what a true friend looks like, because you must remember, this is when friends will have influence, and this is when they will need you to be their best friend, for as a parent you guided them, now as a friend you will influence them. You see, you will be a friend when the time is right; however, don't start the journey as a friend because you may never gain back the parenting respect that is needed to demand certain outcomes early on in their adolescence. As I stated before, parenting is an art form and not a science, so there will be trial and error, mind you; however, I caution you once more to be that parent at the onset, and remember you will always have time to become a friend. And if you do it the right way, you may very well become their best friend and there is absolutely nothing wrong with that.

Let's see what one expert has to say: Joanne Stern Ph.D. From her book: Parenting Is a Contact Sport.

Parent or Friend: Do I Have to Choose?
There's no conflict between being a parent and a friend.

You shouldn't be friends with your kids. What they need is a parent, not another friend. Right?

Wrong. That's a parenting myth that needs to be debunked.

Actually, there's no conflict between being a parent and a friend. And here's why. A parent who is approachable, accessible and has their kids' best interests at heart grows a close bond with them.

We just call that a friendship. And you can set boundaries and have effective discipline- because your kids respect you enough to obey you.

But let me explain to you what I mean when I say you should be friends with your kids. **Your friendship is a caliber higher and a layer deeper than those they have with their peers**. It's a caliber higher because you bring with you knowledge, experience, wisdom, and mature decision making ability. It's a layer deeper because you don't get jealous or competitive with your children and you never abandon or betray them.

Think for a moment about how you are with your kids when they're young. You *are* their friend. You laugh, talk and play games with them and you enjoy each other immensely. And, of course, you still maintain discipline. Your kids benefit immensely from this friendship because it establishes a solid base of trust and respect between you. **Why would you want to back away from or sever that close and positive relationship when they reach the pre-teen and teen years- times when they're struggling with their growth into adulthood and meeting big challenges along**

the way? In fact, these are the times they need your support, your caring and your influence the most.

But, parenting is an art, not a science, and there are several ways you can get off track with them. **Let me give you some tips to help you stay in balance.**

1. **You don't want to become permissive.** Effective parents set boundaries and permissive ones erase those boundaries. You don't hang out with them on Saturday night giggling about their boyfriends, using their slang, dressing like they do and trying to be oh so hip and cool. You don't share inappropriate and intimate details about our life with them just to try to get close to them. You don't give in to them so they will like you. A parent who is also a friend keeps the boundaries crisp and clear, but you let them know-and feel-that you're there with them for the long haul.

2. **You don't want to be distant and aloof.** If you were, you wouldn't get to know them and they wouldn't get to know you. There would be minimal trust between you, and they wouldn't share with you what's happening in their lives, so you would lose your ability to influence and guide them. If you're closed down with them, they'll close down to you. If you don't open up to them and promote mutual sharing, the communication between you will be tense and surface. Communication is a two way street-in any kind of relationship. And it's the bedrock of a relationship. So if you decide to be distant, you have to give up on being close to your kids.

3. **You don't want to be controlling.** When you control, kids tend to rebel. Instead of getting on the inside track with them, they will be out to disobey and get out from under your control. They might rebel openly and loudly by looking for ways to sneak, lie and cover up; to be un-cooperative, to be sullen and to talk back. Or they might rebel

quietly by getting an eating disorder-because you simply cannot control what they put in their mouths or what they don't. Control doesn't feel like respect, and if you don't respect them, you can't expect your kids to respect you.

4. **You don't want to become a helicopter parent.** When you hover over your kids making all their decisions for them, trying to prevent them from making a mistake or-God forbid-failing, you actually damage their self-esteem. They see your hovering as a message that you don't trust them and that you don't believe they can take care of themselves. The more you guide them in decision making, but allow them to make their own-in age appropriate ways-the more mature and wise they become in making good choices. And you want to teach them that failing is okay. It's part of the human experience. You can ask them what decision they made that led to a bad outcome, how could they have handled it better, what they can do to recover and

how you can help. And you can model for them how to deal with mistakes by admitting some of your own. Instead of making them feel belittled, berated, humiliated, put down or stupid, teach them that failure is a learning tool.

So what's the best position to take? Being a parent who is a friend because that's how you help your kids most and that's how you get to be the one they talk to-and listen to-even during the tough times.

So there you have it, an everyday fathers take on parent vs. friend, and a Ph.D. scholar's take, and I must say they are not that off from one another, so my opinion to you would be to take what works for you here and be the best possible father and friend you can be, with the focus always being the betterment of your child, and you staying as a father.

As usual let's find out what the Word says:

Deuteronomy 6:6-9 *And these words that I command you today shall be on your heart. You* *shall teach them diligently to your children, and shall talk of them when you sit in your house, and when you walk by the way, and when you lie down, and when you rise. You shall bind them as a sign on your hand, and they shall be as frontlets between your eyes. You shall write them on the doorposts of your house and on your gates.*

Proverbs 22:6 *Train up a child in the way he should go; even when he is old he will not depart from it.*

Ephesians 6:4 *Fathers, do not provoke your children to anger, but bring them up in the discipline and instruction of the Lord.*

Ephesians 6:1-3 *Children, obey your parents in the Lord, for this is right. "Honor your father and mother" (this is the first commandment with a promise), "that it may go well with you and that you may live long in the land."*

Actually, I didn't really find any Scripture that literally speaks to parent vs. friend; however, the verses I did find do speak to the act of parenting and how children should respect their parents. Madison's mom and I didn't stay together, and we've been divorced for some time now. However, we did choose to raise Madison as a child of God, and I can say by doing so we have been blessed with a wonderful God-fearing, and parent respecting beautiful young lady. Clearly the choice is yours, my question is which will you choose?

Chapter Eight
Consistency through Challenges

With life comes many challenges, and how we face these challenges is mostly based on how we've been equipped, and the tools that we've been given along the way. When you think of the word equipped, you may envision a sports environment where the players are given the proper equipment in order to get out on the grid iron and become successful as a team. The equipment they are given has usually been approved by both the league and the players, and eventually is added to the wording within the Collective Bargaining Agreement (CBA). Once written into the CBA, all players within said league must govern themselves according to the agreement. Meaning they can only wear what has been agreed upon, and if an item that is not agreed upon is worn, the player is fined, or for lack of a better word, punished. The tools they are given are meant to give them the best chance possible at becoming a winner, the greatest opportunity to be successful in their career, and a shot at becoming the best in the world at what they do. Basically, they are given what is needed to be consistent.

In our lives, overcoming challenges is the very thing that makes us stronger; however, it can also be the very thing that takes us out, and for that reason we have learned to equip ourselves with the necessary tools to ready ourselves in the midst of said challenges. We've come to understand that a certain amount of stability and structure is needed to maneuver these rustling waters that we call life. We now know that a certain level of consistency is necessary, and when coupled with organization and structure, we have the chance to become a much more prepared individual while facing life's obstacles. Knowing what we know today, and having lived a bit of life ourselves, we should be that much more prepared as parents to equip our children with the necessary tools to make them far more successful than we ourselves ever were.

However, men if we are not willing to be consistent in our lives, we have no chance of advancing our children's future, as we've failed them by failing ourselves. Growing up, my mom did all that she could to keep our heads above water; however, she had little to no education, so we were given what she felt was a strong foundation, a high level of discipline, and real love; however, solid equipment and the proper tools were not a part of the menu. Due to this lack of the necessary equipment, there was no consistency, and my siblings and I were forced to try things, learn things, and fail at many things which has created major setbacks for a couple of my siblings that just couldn't handle the challenges.

I don't blame my mom's lack of education on whether or not we were able to persevere; however, I do believe that with furthered education, she would've had a better understanding, a deeper resource pool, a stronger mindset, and a much more organized approach in teaching us how to be more consistent in our day-to-day lives. You see in order to lead someone or be in charge of a team, one must learn to be consistent. Consistent in all aspects of life, as this will lead to far more victories and more than likely you will find that you have accomplished life at a much higher level. Now isn't that what you want for yourself and those that are entrusted to your care? It's most definitely what I want for my daughter, and that's why I chose to be consistent, even when she hated me, and believe me, they will hate you, or think they hate you at some point if you are being consistent. Your job is to deal with the momentary outburst and phantom hate that they will muster up and throw at you, for believe you me, if you don't break and you don't give in, you will have developed in your child a winning attitude that will take them to an extreme they could never fathom.

The consistency I'm speaking of is vital, and must take place if we are to be successful in giving our children the best possible chance at success. Look at the top companies in our world today, most are committed to customer service, function with a high level of organization, honor their employees, and operate with a high level of consistency. I take that very same model, include a few of my personal beliefs, and then put it into action in most all aspects of my daily routine. Not only have I been successful in taking my life to a better place; however, it has also made me a more organized, focused, disciplined, and well-rounded individual.

This in large part has created for me a far higher quality of life, a much more common sense approach to things, and the ability to be the type of father that is embedded in his child's future no matter what challenges may come. And come they will my friend in all shapes and sizes, and all forms and fashions. How you've prepared for them will be the big question.

I've had the opportunity to learn a lot by doing; however, had I had the appropriate equipment and tools during my first journey into fatherhood, I know my eldest daughter would've benefited far better than she did, and I apologize deeply to Monique for not being there. Basically, due to my lack of courage and my inability to step up and take on my role in her life, she has had to battle challenge after challenge. This snapshot of my failure is exactly the picture I want to paint in your mind, the picture of a father that was unequipped, full of fear, unorganized, and running towards failure faster than a speedy bullet. Dad apologizes Monique and I pray that I can one day make it up to you.

My present journey into fatherhood has been a far more organized process where I knew I was ready to handle the day to day challenges of being a parent. With this opportunity, I took it upon myself to change things about my life that needed to be changed, and to let go of relationships that were not proactive to being a parent. I basically took on fatherhood as if it was a business, and I put all that I had into making my business successful. I hate to equate raising my child to running my own business; however, if you think about it, how much time does one put into assuring a business is successful? Usually every waking minute of your life, so with a business mindset, I became a father that basically put a parental plan together that was based on being consistent in every aspect.

When you think of starting a business, your first assignment is to produce a business plan, where you are looking at trends and market share, finding startup capital, and training and developing staff. Well as in business, raising your child needs to be planned out thoroughly and you should know and understand that financial stability is of high importance as you will be supporting your child for many years to come. You should also be aware of the trends of the youth where your child will be attending school and spending most of his/her social life. These are all important aspects of youth development, as we all have heard that old adage, you are what you eat. Well if our children are allowed to eat meals of the wrong variety, there will be many more challenges, and if you can stop the threat of unnecessary challenges, do so without hesitation, as there will be enough challenges without allowing those that we can steer clear of.

Challenges that we have no control over will come from all areas of your life, and you will spend many hours dealing with them. It's how you deal with them that will determine the future of your child, so remember as these challenges arise, you are not the essence of what is happening; however, your child's life hangs in the balance, so your decision-making needs to be a thoroughly thought-out process. You've basically lived your life man, you've decided to be a dad, so you now have to put yourself aside and be there to fight off all the negativity that will come with this choice. Things will begin to seemingly fall out of the sky to hinder you, and make you pack it in and run, but you must dig your feet in and fight. That's right, fight for the life of your little ones as they cannot fight for themselves, and this fight will require a father that will not run at the first sign of a challenge; however, he will put his children on his shoulders and stand firm against what will come. That's the spirit you need to combat these challenges, the spirit of a warrior that when night falls, he doesn't turn and run, he ventures deeply in that jungle and fights through the challenges in order to provide for those that God has put under his leadership.

Life's challenges are real, and they can come from places you never thought they would, now add being a parent to the mix, man, if you thought you had challenges before; get ready. I remember being in the hospital when Madison was born, all the joy and jubilation of becoming a father running through me, had me feeling like a king. Well, no sooner than I was being crowned, along came the first challenge in the form of my mother-in-law. You see Madison's mom is Italian, so my being black really didn't sit well with my in-laws;

however, I was not going to let racial discomfort scare me away from my fatherly duties, and with that said I pushed on pass the racial tension and made that day into one of my best ever. I mean the tension from her mom's side of the family was always present, so I learned quickly to deal with it and did not allow it to push me away.

Believe me, if you've never experienced racial tension you have no idea what it can do, but if you have, then you know what I was made to endure, and the challenge it can present within a marriage. The good news is we've come a long way in society today, and there was no way that I was going to allow some old school bottled up racism to impede me from being Madison's father.

And that was just the beginning brothers because the tension of life itself began to hit me with every shot it could, and I stood in there and fought for the life of my daughter through each and every blow. I mean there's the financial challenge where some days you just feel like quitting because you go to the bank and you don't have enough to purchase what is needed to sustain your family. You may even begin to question yourself, asking am I man enough to take on this responsibility of being the head of this family or did I get in over my head? You may start to hear all the naysayers with all their negativity reminding you that you aren't good enough for your daughter, find a job that pays well, or just leave; we will help her mom provide for Madison. I tell you men, be prepared to be kicked while you are down, and to be criticized constantly for every shortcoming in your life. However, you must stay consistent because this is not about you, it is about the life of your precious little one, and if you run, so will she, right into the arms of some loser that will wreak havoc in her life as well as yours.

Remember the winds of change will bring about challenge after challenge, your daughter will hate you, your in-laws will despise you, you will lose jobs, you may go through divorce, you may face racism, and the very ones that are the closest to you, your so-called family, they very well just might abandon you too. But I promise you, if you fall on your knees and ask your heavenly Father to get you through, He will hold you in the palm of His hands and you will prevail.

I was a selfish type, always looking out for me kind of dude when I embarked upon parenthood, and I knew nothing about raising a child; however, for some reason I was made to work with youth that had no one in their lives to nurture them in a way a real parent should. I told myself during those years I would never walk away from my parenting duties ever again, no matter what the circumstance. No matter what challenges may come, I decided to be consistent as a father, I decided that I would make sure that my child would always have what was needed, and that I would always put her needs first. It's not an easy thing to do so I won't sit here and tell you that it is; however, I will tell you it's the right and only thing to do if you want to see your child succeed in the world.

My brother is a minister and I once heard him say while giving a sermon "You can't teach what you don't know, and you can't lead where you don't go." That statement still resonates with me today, for as a father it reminds me that I have to be there for Madison, I have to be the one to teach and lead so that I can be sure that she will know a fathers perspective. A perspective that hopefully one day will aid her in choosing an individual that will continue the good cycle, the cycle that produces men that earn the badge of fatherhood through the same perseverance she witnessed in that guy she calls dad.

Now let's examine some expert opinion from the folks at Hand in Hand Parenting on Consistency in Parenting:

We've all been told, "Kids need consistency!" But what does that mean?

Does it mean that we have to mete out consequences for every one of our children's poor judgment calls? Does it mean that being flexible with them will pamper and spoil them? How can we tell when it's important to be consistent, and when it's not?

I think that the consistency our children need lies in our ability to *think about each situation flexibly*. If they can depend on us to think, rather than react, they have the security they need in the jumble of daily life. When we can treat our children with respect and love, even while saying no to them, we're being *consistently on their side*. That's the consistency that matters.

For instance, take bedtime. A parent can hold to a consistent bedtime on school nights, but loosen that policy for a child's birthday celebration on a school night, when grandparents or cousins are visiting, or on a night when there's a meteor shower that's best observed after 9 pm. That's thinking. That's setting limits well, and making exceptions well. Both the limits and the exceptions reassure a child that he's well loved, and that his parents have his best interests at heart.

Setting family policy is important.

Policies are the expectations we set to guide how we treat one another in the family, and how we take good care of ourselves. Policies express what it means to treat others as we would like to be treated. They also cover things like safety, health, pet care, and as children grow, how money is saved and spent. It's good to include children in the making of policy by having regular family meetings, where everyone, no matter how young, gets to have their say about what would be fair and good.

We communicate good policy best by modeling it. Policies like "We always let one another know where we're going and when we're coming back," or "When you want to borrow something, ask first," sink in when they're quietly followed day by day, by parents with one another, and with their children. Lectures about these expectations don't really help children much. Limits and caring reminders, following Staylistening or Playlistening, do. "Oops! Looks like you took your sister's new gel pen without asking her. Please go and ask her now," gives a child a reasonable expectation. If she can't respond cooperatively, she's not thinking. She's not feeling connected enough to take others into consideration. This is the time to move closer, offer connection, and use Listening Tools to bring the limit, listen, and help your child reconnect.

In a family in which children are treated with respect, they will be helpful by letting parents know when they see *them* crossing policy lines. "Don't talk to me that way, Mommy. There's some mean in your voice," is the kind of reminder that a young child who hasn't been intimidated will give a parent. It's very helpful to have our children help us when they see us being inconsistent and off track. They want us at our best, and so do we!

Focus on connection as you follow through with a limit.

Children need sound policy, lovingly delivered. They never need harshness, but they do need firm boundaries on important issues. They never need lectures, but they will learn much from their parents' example. They never need punishment, but they do sometimes need tighter boundaries until they can laugh and tantrum and cry enough troubles away to feel less threatened and better connected. In the meantime, those tighter boundaries will most certainly trip up big feelings for them. The boundaries aren't punishment. They're recognition that this child can't handle certain situations well yet. For instance, a child who tends to run away from his parents in public might have to stay home while an older child, who doesn't, gets to go with Daddy to the park today. The healing process lies in our ability to *listen* to our children's feelings, so eventually the child can connect in and cooperate more fully. The promise of "There'll be a chance to go to the park with

Daddy another time, when he can help you stay close to him" lets a child know, while he's crying, that he's loved in spite of his difficulties.

With our children and with one another, we need to focus on the high priority issues, and sometimes let the little stuff go, to preserve our own energy. Whether the clothes mom folded are put away by the children is truly less important than whether the siblings pummel one another in a moment of fury. However, a child's refusal to put the folded clothes away might signal the kind of disconnection that can result in a sibling battle ten minutes later. So setting limits about a minor issue might allow a child to cry hard about not wanting to cooperate. When a parent listens, cares, and stays warm but firm with, "I know it's hard. But the clothes need to be put away before anything else happens," a child can cry his edginess away. The connection that the parent's listening brings will head off trouble later.

The kind of consistency a child needs is her parent's fresh thinking.

The consistency a child needs most is her parent's ability to think. When a parent can think, he can tell the difference between a minor goof which barely needs a mention, and a blatant sign that a child is asking for help.

How we parents become more consistently able to think (and love and care, which comes bundled with the ability to think) is by being listened to. When we have the time to talk about how parenting is going for us, and shed the emotional tension that builds up day by day, we have a way to restore our own sense that someone cares about us. Being listened to returns us to our parenting job with less on our minds and more certainty that our children are good people. When we can remember that they're good and that we're good, too, we are better at limits, listening, and caring. We suggest Listening Partnerships, simple but life-changing exchanges of listening that parents can learn do with one another, either in person or by phone.

Here's an example of a parent being consistent in her caring, and flexible about her policy.

A friend of mine was a single mom with one daughter, and was on a very limited budget. The mom was committed to connecting with her daughter through Special Time, and also worked to feed her daughter healthy food. She didn't often allow sugary foods at home. She found that it was easier to say "No" at the store and keep them out than it was to be asked for a treat over and over again throughout the day.

For Special Time one day, her 9-year-old daughter asked her for a trip to the ice cream shop. Her mom asked her what she wanted, and she said, "I want to eat as much ice cream as I want!" This mom thought about it for a moment and said, "Yes! Let's go." Her daughter was thrilled and surprised. She had never before asked to have multiple scoops of ice cream, and never expected her mom to agree!

They went to the shop together, and the mom did her best to be enthusiastic and admiring as her daughter ordered 7 scoops of various flavors, all on one plate. She dug in! Her mom didn't lecture, and didn't warn her that she was going to get sick. She cheered her daughter on.

She figured that in this Special Time, for once in her life, her daughter could try eating ice cream to her heart's content. The mom knew she would set limits later, and figured that if her daughter did suffer ill consequences, she'd learn from it. My friend decided that she wasn't going to spoil the experience in any way. She was going to admire the flavors, enjoy every detail of her daughter's high time at the ice cream shop, and not dilute it with any "parent downers." It was just one time, so it could be glorious.

And my friend noticed, afterward, that her daughter felt closer to her and was more relaxed than she'd been in a long time. The mom figured that she had shown her daughter that she trusted her, and trusted what she wanted for this one time. She showed that she could put aside her usual policies, and let her daughter's wishes come first. It made a difference to allow a special exception. It made a difference to rise above the usual rules, and above her fears of what 7 scoops of ice cream might do. And indeed, no one got sick. Now, many years later, both mother and daughter are healthy, and they're very close.

You see, even the experts talk about policy and flexibility in parenting, just as in the business world. They also mention there being no need to beat your child down physically, as this style of child development can be very detrimental to a child's future and how they survive this life. My mom was a devout believer in punishment and beating our behinds, and not to say we didn't deserve it at times; however, it served to hinder two of my brothers in many ways and they have been stymied by the taking of their manhood caused from the beatings. They have also been made to feel hated and abandoned in many ways, thus rendering them unable to thrive alone and causing them to look to alcohol and drugs for comfort. Choose the style of negativity and brutality, and your children just may go that route as well; however, if you choose a consistent, loving, nurturing style of parenting, the possibility for success in your child's life will be far greater.

Now a bit of biblical guidance on consistency:

1 Corinthians 15:58 ESV
Therefore, my beloved brothers, be steadfast, immovable, always abounding in the work of the Lord, knowing that in the Lord your labor is not in vain.

Galatians 6:9 ESV
And let us not grow weary of doing good, for in due season we will reap, if we do not give up.

Titus 2:7-8 ESV
Show yourself in all respects to be a model of good works, and in your teaching show integrity, dignity, and sound speech that cannot be condemned, so that an opponent may be put to shame, having nothing evil to say about us.

James 1:4 ESV
And let steadfastness have its full effect, that you may be perfect and complete, lacking in nothing.

As you read here you will find that the words consistent or consistency are missing; however, words such as ***steadfast***, ***steadfastness***, and ***all respects*** basically equate to the word consistent. These words all share the same meaning when being used here, basically meaning to stay on track and stay focused. Finally above all else just stay, and be the best possible father you can be, and I promise your child/children will love you to the highest extreme. They won't always like you, however when the rubber meets the road and at the end of the day they will know that you stayed and gave every effort possible to assure they are given the best opportunities in becoming successful in their own lives as responsible citizens that give back, and more than that responsible parents themselves.

Chapter 9
Identity Crisis

Who am I here? One of my favorite lines from a movie I once watched called The Stepfather. The plot was about this psychotic dude that travelled through various cities marrying several ladies, and becoming a stepfather to their children. Basically he eventually got in over his head and fell into an identity crisis and became unable to remember who he was, or what family he was with, and in the end it all worked out to his demise.

In this case the identity crisis I would like to speak to is not that of an adult; however, this identity crisis comes in the form of our children, and please understand me here; it will come. If you take a look back at your adolescence I am sure you will remember a particular time when you struggled with your identity. Whether it was not knowing who your father was, or having a different last name than your other siblings, the crisis was real and we had to find a way to deal with it. Of course our parents wanted nothing to do with the questions that were raised during this crisis, and for reasons such as that, there we were left alone with no answers and a void left in our hearts rendering us even less unsure of whom we were.

I still question many things today about our upbringing, however I am learning to let it go as life has gone on, and my mom will never change her stance on the situation. All she will say is that I am your mom and you didn't need any one else. Well I have to beg to differ, for when these things are left on discussed it can create a major identity crisis, and from said crisis will spawn hatred, anger, and separation of family. I know about this, for I was made to endure Madison's meltdowns and for the most part during these meltdowns I was the scapegoat and often times left hurting and feeling very much alone.

I can recall on several occasions as she went from one identity crisis to the next how often I would be thrown to the curb for reasons that were fabricated, however being that a child is easily influenced Madison took the bait time and time again and as I said daddy became the bad guy. Well daddy learned through each episode that He would have to withstand each onslaught, as

Madison was being influenced by outside forces that she trusted. The trust in those influences can cause your child to lash out at you with a deep cutting anger, that if you are not strong enough in your fatherhood it can very well push you away for life, or even more detrimental cause them to hate you.

Yes, your child's identity crisis if not met head on can leave you feeling like 10 miles of rough road and so disconnected from them that you find yourself drowning in your tears and left alone. This period of time will play a large part in developing in you the strength, the patience, and the love that you will need to lean on to make it through. I can assure you that during these years of their identity crisis you will be made as a father to feel as though you can't do anything right, you're the worst father in the world, and basically we don't need you. Prepare yourselves men for this will be a tough time, and I will encourage you now to understand that they are children and usually when something doesn't go their way you as the father will be the scapegoat. Understand now that this is the nature of the beast, and if you can keep your faith in tact and not allow this temporary transition into young adulthood work its way through, you will be okay, I promise.

I am a living portrait of perseverance when it comes to experiencing this transition in life, for I was made to feel like shit on many occasions, and told I hate you more often than I care to remember. However I chose to not allow this temporary adolescence state of mind send me packing nor hinder me from fulfilling my fatherly duties. Mind you, it wasn't easy and it will be very pain staking; however, the alternative is to stop parenting and they will be left alone, and forever searching to find their identity for the rest of their lives. Again it won't be easy.

Allow me to share with you here a couple of experiences that I dealt with during the identity crisis period in Madison's life where I was made to feel so bad that I felt like ending it because my child hated me and wanted nothing to do with me. Honestly, I didn't want to live anymore on the day my daughter sent me a four page diatribe explaining to me how I had been a horrible dad and that she didn't want to live with me anymore. All I could think of was this was her mother's doing, as the words she wrote resonated her mother's voice completely, and with each word I developed more hate for the both of them. The words cut so deeply that I called my mom crying and as usual she was there for me reassuring me that I was an excellent father, and that someday Madison would come to realize that.

She reminded me of those years when Madi and I were inseparable and how she would never leave my side when we were together. Yes, my mom was there once again to provide that mothers love and reassurance that only she could, and in doing so I was made strong again. My mom went on to advise me to allow Madi her wishes of not wanting to live with me and not wanting to receive any further child support payments if I agreed to their terms. So agreed, I did, and with that we went our separate ways for a couple years with little to no communication.

These were two of the toughest years of my life, as I had always been connected to my daughter and now we were so far apart that it really didn't feel like I had a child. I mean it got to the point where I didn't go to any of her school events, didn't receive cards for my birthday, and more than that she didn't invite me to her high school graduation. Oh don't get me wrong I attended in her support but there was no contact or even a look. I was devastated as I sat there and listened to her talk about her mom and stepdad as if I didn't even exist. My family members were in awe as they sat there wondering what the hell was going on, as I hadn't shared with them the details of mine and Madi's falling out. They immediately (following the ceremony) overwhelmed me with questions regarding the present state of our relationship; however, I chose not to disclose anything as I was highly emotional and didn't want to get into my personal affairs.

Actually it wasn't until that following summer prior to her leaving for college that she finally broke her silence and reached out to me to say goodbye. It was a very emotional meeting, and we were both taken over by tears; however it was at that moment when I realized that my mom was right. I needed to let Madison go and deal with herself, and those she listened to so that she could realize that they too had flaws, and that her father wasn't the monster they had made him out to be. My daughter had finally found herself, and in doing so she realized that her dad was and always had been there for her.

Hear me when I say this men, you have to understand that nothing worth fighting for is ever easy, and that you will be made to look and feel like shit. However, if you are willing to endure for what may be several seasons, and willing to fight for your child during this identity crisis, you will come out on the other side. You cannot allow this period of their development to scare you off because your feelings get hurt or your child believes he/she hates you. Remember, they are having an identity crisis, and it is your job to help them through it. This is the very time that when instead of running away because your feelings got hurt, you should be running next to them helping them establish who they are, and how important it is to fulfill their destiny.

We must not allow the challenges of life to defeat the future we have as fathers, for if we do, we will have relinquished our rights to assuring our children the opportunity for a better life. We will also have failed them and society for we will be responsible for any and all of their destructive behaviors towards mankind. That's right, we all contribute in some way towards society, so in failing our children and fleeing our responsibilities as fathers we will most certainly be adding to society's negative impact; however, if we stay, chances are very likely that their impact will be absolutely positive.

Understand one very important thing here men, this identity crisis situation is real. If our children are not fostered through this time of social challenge, and finding their identity, the percentages for their success become very low. Statistics have shown that when an adolescent is not equipped with a strong identity, they have a far less chance of making it in society. When I think of strong, I think of a man with big muscles, able to handle anything that comes his way. Well guess who that man is for our children, it is you and me, and if our children are to have a strong identity, we as fathers need to be there to help them find it. As I said before, this is not a time to be weak and emotional and make this about you. This is a time to dig in and plant your feet, and proclaim to your child that their daddy isn't going anywhere, and that you are going to be here come hell or high water. This is the time when you are to put on that badge of fatherhood and let the world know, I am here.

Now let's look at this identity crisis from a psychological perspective.

In psychology, the term **identity crisis** (coined by psychologist Erik Erikson) means the failure to achieve ego identity during adolescence.[1][2]

The stage of psychosocial development in which identity crisis may occur is called the Identity Cohesion vs. Role Confusion. During this stage, adolescents are faced with physical growth, sexual maturity, and integrating ideas of themselves and about what others think of them.[3] Adolescents therefore form their self-image and endure the task of resolving the crisis of their basic ego identity. Successful resolution of the crisis depends on one's progress through previous developmental stages, centering on issues such as trust, autonomy, and initiative

Those who emerge from the adolescent stage of personality development with a strong sense of identity are well equipped to face adulthood with confidence and certainty. Sometimes individuals face obstacles that may prevent the development of a strong identity. This sort of unresolved crisis leaves individuals struggling to "find themselves." They may go on to seek a negative identity, which may involve crime or drugs or the inability to make defining choices about the future. "The basic strength that should develop during adolescence is fidelity, which emerges from a cohesive ego identity."[2]

Erikson's own interest in identity began in his childhood. Born Ashkenazic Jewish, Erikson felt that he was an outsider. His later studies of cultural life among the Yurok of northern California and the Sioux of South Dakota helped formalize Erikson's ideas about identity development and identity crisis. Erikson described those going through an identity crisis as exhibiting confusion.[2]

They often seem to have no idea who or what they are, where they belong or where they want to go. They may withdraw from normal life, not taking action or acting as they usually would at work, in their marriage or at school. They may even turn to negative activities, such as crime or drugs, as a way of dealing with identity crisis. To someone having an identity crisis, it is more acceptable to them to have a negative identity than none at all.[2]

Erikson felt that peers have a strong impact on the development of ego identity during adolescence. He believed that association with negative groups such as cults or fanatics could actually "redistrict" the developing ego during this fragile time. The basic strength that Erikson found should develop during adolescence is fidelity, which only emerges from a cohesive ego identity. Fidelity is known to encompass sincerity, genuineness and a sense of duty in our relationships with other people.[2]

Erikson described identity as "a subjective sense as well as an observable quality of personal sameness and continuity, paired with some belief in the sameness and continuity of some shared world image. As a quality of unself-conscious living, this can be gloriously obvious in a young person who has found himself as he has found his communality. In him we see emerge a unique unification of what is irreversibly given—that is, body type and temperament, giftedness and vulnerability, infantile models and acquired ideals—with the open choices provided in available roles, occupational possibilities, values offered, mentors met, friendships made, and first sexual encounters."[4]

Now after having read that statement, I want to ask you: How important do you think it is to be there to assure your child acquires a strong identity? I mean honestly, if we were to take a look back at our very own adolescence, I guarantee you there are siblings of ours that emerged from adolescence with weak identities, and still today they struggle with society and find it hard to survive in this world. I am also willing to bet that if we take a deeper look into their upbringing that they probably come from single parent homes where the dad was just a sperm donor. Don't be that dad, choose to be a father and help establish in your children a strong sense of identity that will instill in them the necessary tools to survive this crazy thing we call life.

Chapter Ten
Spiritual Guidance
Theirs and Yours

Early on in the lives of my siblings and me, my mom made it of the utmost importance to introduce us to a life of faith, which meant we were in Sunday school and church every Sunday. Mind you there was no choice, there was only the every Sunday forced awakening to an awesome breakfast and the words "Get ready for church and y'all better be in your Sunday best." To me church was a fashion show where one could see the latest fashions, as the sharp dressed minister and his first lady pranced about giving instruction and praising God. To my mom, however, it was a foundation building that she felt each of us needed in order to become well-rounded individuals that would first honor God, and that would always honor and respect our parents and other adults.

Back then I had no idea what she was doing; however, over the years I've come to understand and appreciate her efforts, as I've learned to lean on the very faith she introduced me to. I couldn't imagine living today without a relationship with God, as when times get tough and you have no one else to turn too, you can always count on Him. I know, some would say that this is not for them; however I say to that, to each his own, and that those without some type of faith in something are usually lost or mired in so many worldly issues that they just can't seem to get beyond them. My challenge to you here is to give it a try, as it can't hurt and you just might find it to be refreshing, revitalizing, and life-changing.

You see if you are never introduced to something, you may never know what it's like, so if you have never had the opportunity to develop a faith life, all I am asking is that you give it a try. What do you have to lose that you haven't lost already? Who knows you just may find that a faith life is exactly what you've been missing. Again I won't sit here and make any promises to you about how much better your life will be if you become a Christian; however, I will share with you some of my experiences and how my relationship with God has helped me through them. I will also share my thoughts on how introducing your child to Christ can be of a great benefit in the maturation process, and instill in them many positive attributes. I mean look at the alternative, you can allow this world to be their foundation and hope for the best, or you can choose to do nothing and watch your child fight for survival in this dog eat dog world where most people are about only themselves. The choice is yours to make, all I am asking is that you be open-minded, and that you put your child's life first. My mom did, and I know that I am a much better person because of it.

You see for me guys, it was clear that once I became a young man old enough to understand what having a relationship with Christ was really about, it was a no brainer, and the choice was simple. I chose God. One Sunday morning while attending service, I was approached by a woman that professed to me and my best friend that the two of us were running from the fire, and that God had work for us to do. That was the day that I as a 16-year-old young man joined Emmanuel Baptist Church in San Jose, California and began my personal relationship with Christ. Although my mom had introduced me to the church at a very young age, there was never really a connection, and it wasn't until I became a teenager that I begin to venture out and learn more.

Since that day (for the most part) my life has been in and out of the church, however after being given the second opportunity to be a father my relationship with Christ has been constant, and my faith has grown immensely. Actually it was though this faith Madison's mom was able to conceive her, as we were told that chances were quite low due to blockage in her tubes. However, the God that we serve heard our prayers and entrusted us with a beautiful baby girl, and we promised Him that we would give her back. That's right, Madison's mom and I got on our knees together and prayed to God that if He would give us a child, we would honor Him by making sure that child would also know and honor Him. It was an easy decision, as we both were then and still are today grounded in our faith, and awesome parents to Madison.

I knew that with the promise came much responsibility to me as a father, and that I would have to make changes in my life to take on such a responsibility. Some of the changes were tough, and sometimes met with reluctance. Some never came, and probably had a lot to do with Madison's mom and me divorcing. Yes we divorced; however, we never wavered from keeping Madison in God's Hands, as we both understood the commitment we made. It came to a point where we rarely agreed on much; however, usually when it came to our daughter we were pretty much on the same page. We both understood the need for a strong foundation and a faith-based life, so Madison would be introduced to Christianity early on; as a matter of fact she attended a private Christian school from pre-K through high school. Talk about commitment right?

Please understand this was our commitment to Madison; however, your commitment may not include private school as neither me, nor her mom was given that opportunity when we grew up. One thing about life I've learned is that you have to play with the hand you've been dealt, and at whatever level that is, we should be willing to sacrifice for those that are entrusted to us. Sending Madison to a private Christian school was a huge sacrifice for us; however, once again there was that promise and in no way, shape, or form would we be breaking it. I know there's the old saying, promises are made to be broken; however, when that promise is made to God and includes the future of your child, I believe one holds himself a bit more accountable to seeing it through.

Seeing it through won't be easy because you are a Christian, as you won't wake up one morning and find life to be any easier, but you will have a new found spirit, a different outlook, and a sense of joy knowing God is with you. I mean don't get me wrong, as I stated earlier, some things about me changed, and in some areas I was still being challenged. You have to understand here we will remain human, and being human we are still tempted daily. The thing is as a human once you accept Christ you should have the courage and strength to fight the temptations as they come. You won't always win, but I promise you this you will get stronger and you will have victories. Have I won every battle? Hell no, but believe you me had I not had any faith in God at all I'd more than likely be dead by now.

Let me share with you here a little about how good God has been to me even though there were times when He should've punished me. That's right there were times when He should've left me alone to deal with my evil ways, however He chose to stay with me and love me when I couldn't love myself. He chose to stay with me through the bad times when most everyone else was nowhere to be found. Believe me I was not a very nice person at times and I burned some bridges and left many people hurting in the wake of my destruction. The one constant however was the love and forgiveness of our Heavenly Father, and I thank Him for it daily.

You see I wasn't always this loving person, awesome father, and big hearted passionate guy that loves giving back to society. I've done my share of bad, and I've wreaked some havoc on many occasions. My worst day was the day I chose to have an affair on Madison's mom.
At the time it happened, it didn't feel bad at all, however, the life I lived afterward was devastating, and it changed the course of several other lives,

destroyed my family, and more than that, it severed the love and trust my daughter had in me. This was a time when I put myself before God and my family, but at no time did He ever leave me. As a matter of fact, He was my strength, and He forgave me when no one else would. How does that work you ask? I don't know, but I do know it's a great feeling knowing that my God is far better to me than I could ever be to myself. I was at a very low place in my life, and I couldn't even look at myself, but there He was to pick me up and forgive me. That's why I am glad that I made that decision when I was 16-years-old. You see most people won't forgive you the way God does, as even still today, Madison's mom can't stand me, and honestly I kind of understand where she's coming from. I never personally apologized to her the way a real man should; however, I most certainly have spent much time on my knees asking for forgiveness. It's not in the heart of man to forgive so easily, and it's most certainly not in the heart of a scorned woman. I hate that it ended in such a way, and I am very sorry for being the reason Madi didn't have both her biological parents under one roof, however once again because of our faith we endured.

That same faith and relationship with Christ that was instilled into Madison as a child, is the very thing that got her through as well. You see had she not been introduced to it, she and I may not be where we are today, because at some point I knew she would have to lean on her own understanding and not that of the background voices. That's right, the same voices that as children we heard, and in hearing those voices, we formed many opinions that we found later on in life to be misleading, for as a child we are easily misled. However, if there has been instilled in you a sense of faith and a relationship with God has been formed, at some point you will mature and come to realize we each have a life to live, and with that life will come challenges.

How each of us responds to these challenges will play a major role in the development and outcomes for those in our circles. I chose to include God as my strength as I endured the challenges and struggles of life, and I also chose to introduce my Madison to that same God. Your choices are yours to make, and I will caution you here for this world can be very tough, judgmental, and unforgiving. Would you rather give your child the foundation needed to endure these challenges, or leave them alone to face these adversities by themselves with no faith or a relationship with God that teaches them to be responsible, respectful, and more importantly honest? That's right, these are the characteristics our children will gain from developing a relationship with Christ, and I've seen firsthand the positive outcomes.

Again it's the life my mom chose for us, and it's the life we chose for Madison, and I am a living witness that my life and Madison's have been a blessing to others, as we have been so blessed ourselves, the only logical choice is to keep the blessings going. I tell you men I could've never lived this life without my relationship with God. Hold on, allow me to rephrase that because you can live a life without a relationship with God, so what I meant to say is that I am very happy that I chose to have a relationship with Christ, and I am even happier that my daughter did. Because you see without it I am nothing, however, just as Philippians 4:13 states "I can do all things through Christ who strengthens me."

The folks at Got Questions?.org had this to say about what it means to have a personal relationship with God.

Question: "What does it mean to have a personal relationship with God?"

Answer: Having a personal relationship with God begins the moment we realize our need for Him, admit we are sinners, and in faith receive Jesus Christ as Savior. God, our heavenly Father, has always desired to be close to us, to have a relationship with us. Before Adam sinned in the Garden of Eden (Genesis chapter 3), both he and Eve knew God on an intimate, personal level. They walked with Him in the garden and talked directly to Him. Due to the sin of man, we became separated and disconnected from God.

What many people do not know, realize, or care about, is that Jesus gave us the most amazing gift— the opportunity to spend eternity with God if we trust in Him. "For the wages of sin is death, but the gift of God is eternal life in Christ Jesus our Lord" (Romans 6:23). God became a human being in the Person of Jesus Christ to take on our sin, be killed, and then be raised to life again, proving His victory over sin and death. "Therefore, there is now no condemnation for those who are in Christ Jesus" (Romans 8:1). If we accept this gift, we have become acceptable to God and can have a relationship with Him.

Having a personal relationship with God means we should include God in our daily lives. We should pray to Him, read His word, and meditate on verses in an effort to get to know Him better. We should pray for wisdom (James 1:5), which is the most valuable asset we could ever have. We should take our requests to Him, asking in Jesus' name (John 15:16). Jesus is the one who loves us enough to give His life for us (Romans 5:8), and He is the one who bridged the gap between us and God.

The Holy Spirit has been given to us as our Counselor. "If you love me, you will obey what I command. And I will ask the Father, and he will give you another Counselor to be with you forever—the Spirit of truth. The world cannot accept him, because it neither sees him nor knows him. But you know him, for he lives with you and will be in you" (John 14:15-17). Jesus said this before He died, and after He died, the Holy Spirit became available to all who earnestly seek to receive Him. He is the one who lives in the hearts of believers and never leaves. He counsels us, teaches us truths, and changes our hearts. Without this divine Holy Spirit, we would not have the ability to fight against evil and temptations. But since we do have Him, we begin to produce the fruit that comes from allowing the Spirit to control us: love, joy, peace, patience, kindness, goodness, faithfulness, gentleness, and self-control (Galatians 5:22-23).

This personal relationship with God is not as hard to find as we might think, and there is no mysterious formula for getting it. As soon as we become children of God, we receive the Holy Spirit, who will begin to work on our hearts. We should pray without ceasing, read the Bible, and join a Bible-believing church; all these things will help us to grow spiritually. Trusting in God to get us through each day and believing that He is our sustainer is the way to have a relationship with Him. Although we may not see changes immediately, we will begin to see them over time, and all the truths will become clear.

Wow, I mean after hearing what you just read, if you haven't developed a relationship with God, now's the time to do it, as it's never too late. You, your family, and your community deserve the opportunity to become better, because when you choose to have this relationship, everyone wins. Your family gets a husband and father with a heart for God, and your community gets a family with a new found love and respect for man that will break down racial tension, hatred, and all negative things that will try to consume us and work towards destroying all that God has meant for good.

Again the choice is yours, and neither I nor anyone else should ever judge you, for I know for a fact that I'm a sinner that has fallen short in many ways; however, the good news is God has forgiven me and He will forgive you as well. The Bible describes faith as follows in Hebrews 11:1; "Now Faith is the substance of things hoped for, and the evidence of things not seen." I chose faith for my family. What will you choose?

Afterword

Throughout history dads have been labeled as the head of the household, the provider, and the man in charge. They weren't really known to be loving, compassionate, or the parent children looked to when life got tough. Oftentimes, dad was the parent that ran off and shirked his responsibilities to the family, more often than not it was to find his next victim to impregnate and leave abandoned with yet another fatherless child. This type of behavior, these senseless acts of irresponsible promiscuity have got to stop. We as men have got to change our mindset, and come to understand that our most precious commodity in this world is our children, and if we don't step up as fathers they will have no future.

Every time a father leaves a household and decides he can't live up to his responsibilities, chances are much higher that the children will drop out of school, get into drugs, commit a crime, and more than likely end up in the criminal justice system. In today's society, the dad's role is far more important than history has shown, as in most cases; it is the father that is spending the majority of quality time. With life ever changing so too has the role of the father in the family. Today's' dad is looked at as cool, and most of the time the parent that the children want to hang out with. Will you be there for them?

Will you be there for them when they run across that finish line, or catch the game-winning touchdown during the big game? How about when they pass or fail their driving test and they look for dad to either celebrate with or console them, will you be there? Tell me will you be there to share with them that big moment when they walk across that stage graduating from high school armed and ready to take on the next major chapter of their life? Will they have to look for you, or will you be there right out in front just like always?

Its decision time dads, and you need to know that when you make this decision there are lives hanging in the balance. Lives that have been entrusted to you and that are now looking to you for guidance, support, love, discipline, and the ability to see through to fruition the responsibility of being their father. That's all they really want a father, a father that will show them that he is going to stay come hell or high water. He is not going to run because he and mom divorces, or he loses a job, or because grandma thinks he's a loser. They need a father that is going to stay no matter what flaws he comes with. The flaws are what make us human, and in being human we are not perfect.

Nothing about parenting is perfect, however it's all about persistence and if you remain persistent in the life of your children as their father I promise you they will be much better off for it, as will you. Your relationship will have a bond that can never be broken, and your children will have a respect for their father that will last a lifetime. You see the thing about being a father isn't worrying about whether they love you, or were you too hard on them. That's not it at all; the main thing is again that you are persistent; persistent with your love, discipline, guidelines and rules, and staying. You can walk out on many things in life, your wife, your job, your friends, your church, and just about anything else you want to.

However, let me say this, it takes a low life coward with no self-respect to walk out on a child. That's right, only a coward would have the nerve to walk out on a helpless, defenseless, needy little individual that not once asked to be brought here. We have no right to stand here and decide that we will leave fatherless babies in the wake of our very own destruction. They did nothing to deserve your wrath, and they absolutely shouldn't have to suffer due to your inability to be a man. If you know that you are a coward and you always run at the first sign of responsibility, then by no means should you even broach the thought of fatherhood, and that's okay. Fatherhood is a job for real men, real men that possess the intestinal fortitude to see his responsibilities through to fruition.

I mean come on fellas, wouldn't you agree that we have enough deadbeat dads running around shirking their fatherly responsibilities. Isn't it time to move the needle in the other direction so the statistics speak to fathers in a positive light? Then join me in promoting positive fathers, and being that change they want, and so badly need to see. Let's take strides together towards developing resources for those of us that are finding it tough to meet the challenges of being a father, and let's make a vow to one another that wherever there is a father in need, there will be a brother there to help with that need.

This isn't a game mind you, and as I stated earlier, lives hang in the balance. We can look at the statistics all day, and I assure you the success rate for a fatherless child are far lower than that of a child where the father was present. There you have it, your child's success lies in you being there and taking on your role. Will you hinder, or help them?

Let's look at some statistics:

FATHERLESS STATS

1. 23.6% of US children (17.4 million) lived in father absent homes in 2014.

[US Census Bureau, 2015] Living arrangements of children under 18 years and marital status of parents, by age, sex, race, and Hispanic origin and selected characteristics of the child for all children: 2014. Washington, D.C.: U.S. Census Bureau.

2. In 2011, children living in female-headed homes with no spouse present had a poverty rate of 47.6%. This is over four times the rate for children living in married couple families.

[Source: U.S. Department of Health & Human Services (2012). Information on poverty and income statistics: A summary of 2012 current population survey data. Retrieved from: http://aspe.hhs.gov/hsp/12/PovertyAndIncomeEst/ib.cfm]

3. A study of 1,397,801 infants in Florida evaluated how a lack of father involvement impacts

infant mortality. A lack of father involvement was linked to earlier births as well as lower birth weights. Researchers also found that father absence increases the risk of infant mortality, and that the mortality rate for infants within the first 28 days of life is four times higher for those with absent fathers than those with
involved fathers. Paternal absence is also found to increase black/white infant mortality almost four-fold.

[Source: Alio, A. P., Mbah, A. K., Kornosky, J. L., Washington, D., Marty, P. J., & Salihu, H. M. (2011). Assessing the impact of paternal involvement on Racial/Ethnic disparities in infant mortality rates. Journal of Community Health, 36(1), 63-68.]

4. A study of 263 13- to 18-year-old adolescent women seeking psychological services found that the adolescents from father-absent homes were 3.5 times more likely to experience pregnancy than were adolescents from father-present homes. Moreover, the rate of pregnancy among adolescents from father absent homes was 17.4% compared to a four (4) percent rate in the general adolescent population.

[Source: Lang, D. L., Rieckmann, T., DiClemente, R. J., Crosby, R. A., Brown, L. K., & Donenberg, G. R.

(2013). Multi-level factors associated with pregnancy among urban adolescent women seeking psychological services. Journal of Urban Health, 90, 212-223.]

5. A study of 1,618 Latina high school students found that lower perceived father support is a predictor of suicidal ideation and behavior.

[Source: De Luca, S. M., Wyman, P., & Warren, K. (2012). Latina adolescent suicide ideations and attempts: Associations with connectedness to parents, peers, and teachers. Suicide and Life-Threat Behavior, 42, 672-683.]

6. Disengaged and remote interactions of fathers with infants is a predictor of early behavior problems in children and can lead to externalizing behaviors in children as early as age 1.

[Source: Ramchandani, P. G., Domoney, J., Sethna, V., Psychogiou, L., Vlachos, H. and Murray, L. (2013). Do early father–infant interactions predict the onset of externalising behaviours in young children? Findings from a longitudinal cohort study. Journal of Child Psychology and Psychiatry, 54, 56–64.]

7. Researchers using secondary data from the Interuniversity Consortium for Political and Social Research examined gun carrying and drug trafficking in young men, linking father absence to the likelihood of engaging in these behaviors. Results from a sample of 835 juvenile male inmates found that father absence was the only disadvantage on the individual level with significant effects on gun carrying, drug trafficking, and co-occurring behavior. Individuals from father absent homes were found to be 279% more likely to carry guns and deal drugs than peers living with their fathers.

[Source: Allen, A. N., & Lo, C. C. (2012). Drugs, guns, and disadvantaged youths: Co-occurring behavior and the code of the street. Crime & Delinquency, 58(6), 932-953.]

8. A study of the relationship between father absence and lower educational attainment for African American females found that a longer duration of father absence is a predictive factor for lower educational success. Researchers discovered that longer duration of father absence often leads to lower income and family economic stress, which puts young women at risk for lower educational achievement.

[Source: Gillette, M. T., & Gudmunson, C. G. (2014). Processes linking father absence to educational attainment among African American females. Journal of Research on Adolescence, 24(2), 309-321.]

9. Children with negative attitudes about school and their teachers experienced avoidance and ambivalence with their fathers. On the other hand, children with a secure attachment to their father and whose father was involved had a higher academic self-concept. The father-child attachment was more associated with the child's social-emotional school outcomes than their academic achievement.

[Source: Newland, L., Chen, H., & Coyl-Shepherd, D. (2013). Associations among father beliefs, perceptions, life context, involvement, child attachment and school outcomes in the U.S. and Taiwan. Fathering, 11, 3-30.]

10. Father involvement is related to positive cognitive, developmental, and socio-behavioral child outcomes, such as improved weight gain in preterm infants, improved breastfeeding rates, higher receptive language skills, and higher academic achievement.

[Source: Garfield, C. F., & Isacco, A. (2006). Fathers and the well-child visit, Pediatrics, 117, 637-645.]

11. According to the Bureau of Justice Statistics, the number of children with an incarcerated father grew 79% between 1991 and 2007. Black fathers accounted for nearly half (46%) of all children with an incarcerated father.

[Source: Glaze, L.E., & Maruschak, L.M. (2010). Parents in prison and their minor children. Washington, D.C.: Bureau of Justice Statistics.]

12. Fifty-five (55.2) percent of WIC recipients are raised by single-mothers, 48.2% of all Head Start recipients are from father-absent homes, and 37% of public assistance and Section 8 housing are female-headed households.

[Source: Nock, S.L, Einolf, C.J. (2008). The one hundred billion dollar man: the annual public costs of father absence. Germantown, MD: National Fatherhood Initiative.]

More Data on the Extent of Fatherlessness

- **An estimated 24.7 million children (33%) live absent their biological father.**
  Source: U.S. Census Bureau, Current Population Survey, "Living Arrangements of Children under 18 Years/1 and Marital Status of Parents by Age, Sex, Race, and Hispanic Origin/2 and Selected Characteristics of the Child for all Children 2010." Table C3. Internet Release Date November, 2010.

- **Of students in grades 1 through 12, 39 percent (17.7 million) live in homes absent their biological fathers.**
  Source: Nord, Christine Winquist, and Jerry West. *Fathers' and Mothers' Involvement in their Children's Schools by Family Type and Resident Status.* Table 1. (NCES 2001-032). Washington, DC: U.S. Dept. of Education, National Center of Education Statistics, 2001.

- **57.6% of black children, 31.2% of Hispanic children, and 20.7% of white children are living absent their biological fathers.**
  Source: *Family Structure and Children's Living Arrangements 2012.* Current

Population Report. U.S. Census Bureau July 1, 2012.

- **According to 72.2 % of the U.S. population, fatherlessness is the most significant family or social problem facing America.** Source: National Center for Fathering, Fathering in America Poll, January, 1999.

Trended Data

- Among children who were part of the "post-war generation," 87.7% grew up with two biological parents who were married to each other. Today only 68.1% will spend their entire childhood in an intact family.
  Source: U.S. Census Bureau. "Living Arrangements of Children Under 18 Years Old: 1960 to Present". U.S. Census Bureau July 1, 2012.http://www.census.gov/population/socdemo/hh-fam/ch5.xls

- With the increasing number of premarital births and a continuing high divorce rate, the proportion of children living with just one parent rose from 9.1% in 1960 to 20.7% in 2012. Currently, 55.1% of all black children, 31.1% of all Hispanic children, and 20.7% of all white children are living in

single-parent homes.
Source: U.S. Census Bureau. "Living Arrangements of Children Under 18 Years Old: 1960 to Present". U.S. Census Bureau July 1, 2012. http://www.census.gov/population/socdemo/hh-fam/ch5.xls

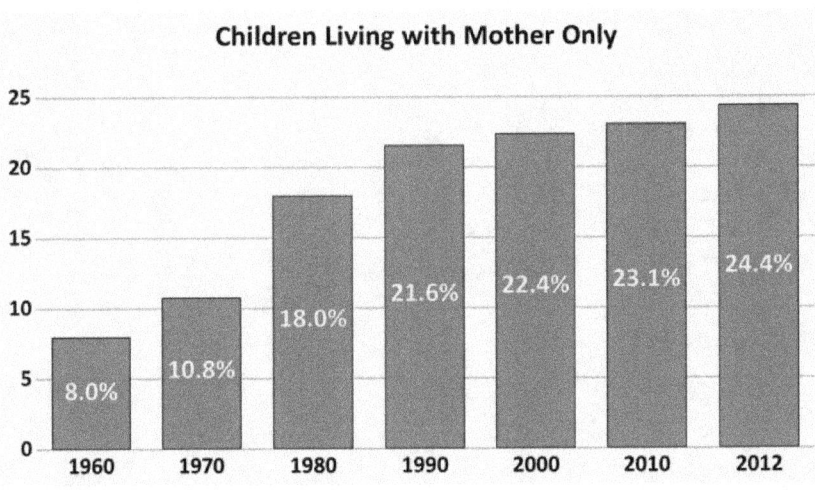

- Source: Census Bureau. "Living Arrangements of Children Under 18 Years Old: 1960 to Present." U.S. Census Bureau, July 1, 2012. http://www.census.gov/population/socdemo/hh-fam/ch5.xls

- White children born in the 1950-1954 period spent only 8% of their childhood with just one parent; black children spent 22%. Of those born in 1980, by one estimate, white children can be expected to spend 31% of their childhood years with one parent, and black children 59%.
Source: Popenoe, David. *Life Without Father* (New York: Simon and Schuster, 1996), 23.

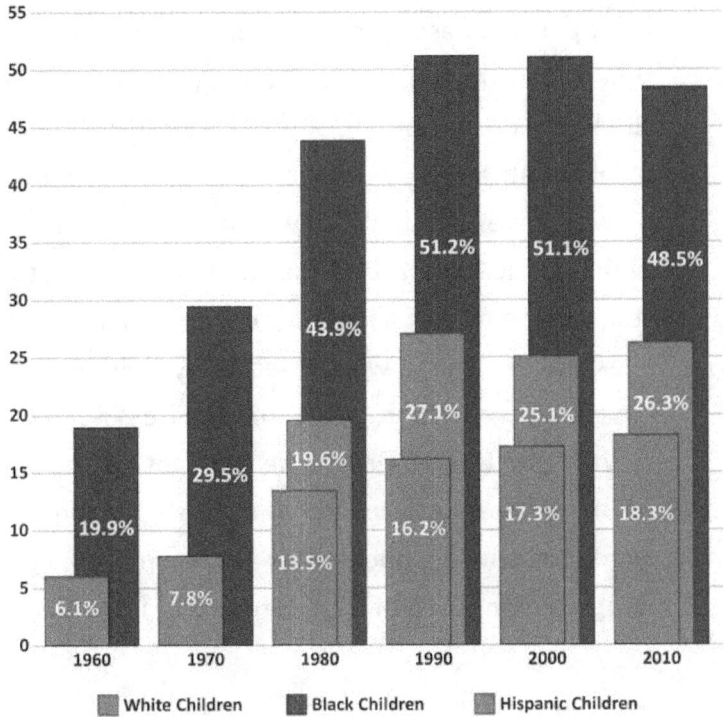

- Source: US Census Bureau, "Living Arrangements of Children Under 18": Tables –CH-2, CH-3, CH-4. 1960 – Present. U.S. Census Bureau July 1, 2012.

The numbers are staggering, and they've for the most part increased steadily year after year. The time is now men, as we can no longer stand on the sidelines and do nothing about this pandemic of faceless fathers in our society. The battle can only be won if we as fathers are willing to step up in faith and face this monster as men, men willing to stand in the face of adversity, look it straight in the eyes and proclaim, I will not leave my child, for I have seen the man in the mirror and he is not a coward. He is a father, and he will fight for the future of those which God has entrusted in him. Fight I tell you, as though your very own life depended on it. Fight for the future of fathers.

Now

Go Find that same Mirror

And take another look...

Acknowledgments

First and foremost, I would like to thank God for giving me the guidance, will, and courage to write this book. I also want to thank my family and all those in my life that have supported, listened, and prayed for me while I have lived this wonderful life and given back as often as I could. I wrote this book with the mindset that half of all sales would go into my non-profit organization the SACTO Foundation (Saving a Child through Opportunity), and I stand on my word. I'd like to thank the loves of my life, my mom Jessie Rosette, and my daughter Madison McPhearson.

Mom you gave me life, and you guided me through my formative years with God, love, and discipline. I will always love you, and you will forever stay in my heart. Thank you so much. Now to my lovely daughter and best friend Madison, you were my inspiration for this wonderful book, and being your father has been the greatest part of my life. You are beautiful, loving, strong, and you possess the heart of a true giver. You are going to make someone a wonderful wife, and be an absolutely great mom. I am both proud and honored to be a father to such a hardworking, and caring young lady. You are the wind beneath dad's wings and I will love you forever.

Bibliography

Levin, Barack, Five things to prepare for before you become a father.

Nerburn, Kent, A changing world.

Abdul-Jabbar, Kareem, 20 things boys can do to become a man.

Parenting.com, Why kids need their dads.

Drexler, Peggy, Raising boys without men.

Lund, Mary, Challenges fathers face after divorce.

The Temptations, My papa was a rolling stone.

Stern, Joanne P.H.D., Parenting is a contact sport.

Hand in hand parenting, Consistency in parenting.

Erikson, Erik, Adolescent identity crisis.

Gotquestions?.org, What it means to have a personal relationship with God.

Fatherhoodfactor.com, Fatherless statistics.

National Center for Fathers, Data on the extent of fatherlessness.

Bible verses, From the King James and English Standards Versions.

The Author
Rick McPhearson

Rick McPhearson has worked extensively in community based organizations with a diverse group of youth whose ages range from adolescence to adulthood. As The S.A.C.T.O Foundations Founder and CEO he is dedicated to assisting in the process of educating humanity to promote understanding and awareness affecting the future of communities in general.

Realizing his passion for writing through becoming a successful grant writer, Rick decided to take his writing skills to the next level, and in doing so he has put together this masterpiece titled The Future of Fathers. His hope is that it serves as a lifeline to dads from every walk of life in helping them to achieve the ultimate attribute in fathering, the honorable badge of fatherhood.

Here's to hoping you enjoyed the read, and to hoping that you saw a change upon taking that last glance in that mirror.

www.ingramcontent.com/pod-product-compliance
Lightning Source LLC
Chambersburg PA
CBHW071920290426
44110CB00013B/1424